'Til I Come Marching Home

'Til I Come Marching Home
A Brief History of American Women in World War II

By C. Kay Larson
With a Foreword by John Eisenhower

Information & Inspiration
The
MINERVA
Center
Women & the Military

Pasadena, Maryland

International Standard Book Number 0-9634895-2-6
Library of Congress Catalog Card Number 95-81150

Production Editor   Debra E. Morgenstern
Copy Editor   Eleanor H. Stoddard

cover photograph: AP/ Wide World Photos

50th Anniversary Special Prepublication Printing

CONTENTS

FOREWORD

In the early days of the Second World War, Colonel Oveta Culp Hobby, commanding officer of the WAAC, made a visit to Europe to check on the performance of the adventurous young women who had come to do their parts in the European Theater. They had been sent to perform whatever duties were assigned to them.

In the course of her visit to the ETO, Colonel Hobby paid a courtesy call on the Supreme Commander, General Dwight D. Eisenhower. The visit went well. General Eisenhower expressed complete satisfaction with the work that Colonel Hobby's trainees were doing in Europe. The visit over, the two went down the hall to leave the building.

When the elevator reached the ground floor, General Eisenhower motioned Colonel Hobby to go ahead out the door. To his astonishment, she refused, telling him nicely to go ahead of her. For a while he insisted, his officer and gentleman upbringing making it mandatory that "ladies go first." But Colonel Hobby was adamant. Military status took precedence, she insisted, over the normal courtesies that were observed in civilian life. General Eisenhower, knowing when he was defeated, went ahead. Colonel Hobby had established that her WAACs were soldiers first, women second.

This incident, small as it was, symbolized the task that military women faced in establishing themselves as full-fledged members of America's fighting team. But that they became, as evidenced by the hundreds of medals and commendations they earned. Their contributions were equalled by those of women in industry, who helped produce the great quantities of weapons so necessary for victory. "Rosie the Riveter" has become part of our lore, even our language. Together the women in the armed forces and in industry proved the immense worth of that vast pool of dedicated and energetic people who set the stage for the increased role that women play in defending America today. Just like the vote, it is coming to be recognized that the role they play is a part of citizenship.

My congratulations on the publication of this book, which tells the story of the first efforts of those pioneers.

John Eisenhower

LIST OF ILLUSTRATIONS

INTRODUCTION

The idea for this book first suggested itself several years ago when my friend, Judith Harlan, showed me letters Lt. Evelyn Orth, Army Nurse Corps, wrote her mother, Hazel Yorke Valley, during World War II. She found them when going through her mother's effects after her death. At that point, I had been researching women in the Civil War for some time. What surprised me was Orth's reference to having lived in tents in Belgium during the 1944-45 winter. My parents' generation had fought the war. My mother had been a nurse and worked at a civilian hospital while her first husband was in the Navy. I grew up watching World War II movies on late night television during summers off from school. So I was sensitive both to some of the gruesome facts of a nursing career and to the sacrifices my parent's generation had made. Within that context, however, my image of World War II nursing was of women working in base hospitals far from the front lines. I saw them in white uniforms which they could keep clean, or at least they had the opportunity for changes. When I read the Orth letters, I said to myself, perhaps like the Civil War ones, World War II nurses lived in field conditions similar to those of the men and were real "combat" nurses.

One question I asked myself was why hadn't I known more about nursing then? The main answer is that although many memoirs have been written and nurses wrote letters home, much of this information is generally unavailable. The number of women's wartime memoirs was not that great. Many that have been published have been in circulation only since the mid-1980s. With a few exceptions, they cannot be found in bookstores. To date, the best outlet is the Women in Military Service for America Memorial "bookshelf."

When the World War II commemoration activities got underway, I became involved through the Coast Guard Auxiliary. I felt that as I was knowledgeable about the Civil War women, it was incumbent upon me to research also the roles of World War II women. Doris Weatherford's book, *American Women and World War II* and unexpected findings regarding women which resulted from my Auxiliary research made me believe that a lot of exciting material was "out there" but few had looked for it.

In doing research for this book, I was confronted with the lack of information from the services and a dissatisfaction with published sources. There is no one Army history of World War II nursing, although Judith Bellafaire's pamphlet published by the U.S. Army Center of Military History is very valuable. Public libraries would not have the history of each service and these deal primarily with administrative history.

Another type of history features collections of women's letters. The problem with this genre is that history-by-anecdote can offer skewed evidence from which to determine trends and conclusions. Often these collections are catch-as-catch-can and the women who were doing the most dramatic things, such as a nurse on Sicily working twelve-hour days, may not have had the energy to write home often.

Most sources do not give enough meaning to the women's work. As a hypothetical example, in a published letter, a nurse on Saipan might write home that she has dengue fever. What she may not say is that there is an epidemic of it there. Even the Army WAC histories do not discuss the extent of the V-1 and V-2 bombings which the women endured in London. Many of the women's jobs required repetitive, detailed work, yet little mention is made of the exhaustion constant attention to detail produces or the consequences of errors. One of the WAVES' jobs was to produce navigation charts. Wrong numbers recorded for water depths could ground warships.

There are other limitations to individual history or anecdotal sources. If only they are accessed, major activities, important figures, and scattered heroines may be missed. For instance, the work of the women in the Civil Air Patrol has gone largely unrecognized.

Reliance on memoirs and unpublished sources will also not necessarily capture women's recognized achievements. The reason I relied on *The New York Times* articles for a good deal of material was that they recorded these. In spite of a general climate of discrimination, as today, during World War II, the strict military rules worked for the women. When they achieved, they were rewarded. Everyone needs heroes and victors, and to date women have been afforded few. This has not been because they have not existed, but because not enough people have publicized them.

In writing this book, the other approach I took was to follow trends I had identified from past wars. As Alexis de Tocqueville and other foreigners have noted, American women have always been intrepid travelers. So they would have been where the war broke out when it did and would have left the United States early to participate in it. Thus, we have the women doctors in England and the resistance workers. Secondly, women would have been active in home defense. The historical image of the frontier woman holding the cabin is a strong one. So I looked for women involved in civil defense work.

Then there is the paradox that the exigencies of war usually demand more of women than what regulations state or what politicians spout. So we find the teenagers spotting planes and flight nurses taking survival training. To find out what women do in war, one must also look at what they do "in the field" in war, as even with the men field conditions may not be the same as training ones, and regulations may be disregarded there.

Other aspects I tried to highlight were as critical incidents and roles. Although history may in hindsight appear as a *fait accompli*, when events are unfolding, participants are afforded choices. The decisions different people make at different times set the course of history. It is not just "great men" or vast numbers of people who determine events. The actions and decisions of individuals holding critical positions can have vast consequences. So even though women did not formulate military strategy, more than a few held critical positions. For women in war, one of their most crucial roles has often been in the area of intelligence. Women make good spies and analysts because of their educational levels and social skills, and because men often underestimate them. So we find Amy Elizabeth Thorpe and Corp. Ginny Johnston making critical intelligence contributions.

Other critical roles, both civilian and military, women played were on the home front, and I tried to bring more meaning to their jobs. More meaning needs to be given to their combined overall role. As an Army pamphlet, "Defense of the Americas," states, "In a sense this campaign was the most important of the entire war, for success in securing the nation proper from external attack was the foundation for Allied victory. Secure from outside attack, the nation built armed forces capable of global action and developed, manufactured, and distributed the modern weapons to equip both these forces and those of America's Allies." Although America's wartime productive capacity is well known, the actual astounding numbers are not. The United States turned out 88,410 tanks to Germany's 46,857. A larger ratio held in aircraft: 283,230 to 107,245. From 1942 to 1945, Japan built only thirteen aircraft carriers; American shipyards launched 137. From 1941 on, military chiefs made American mobilization, logistical support, and overseas combat priorities over passive continental defense. At the height of the Army's continental defense efforts in 1943, there were only 185,000 combat troops stationed in the States, mostly manning coastal artillery and antiaircraft installations. Shore and port protection was largely a Coast Guard function. From the very start of the war, all the services began to strip the United States of combat units and send them overseas, especially after 1943.

In reading the Third District Coast Guard magazine for 1945, one is struck by the fact that almost all the articles are about SPARs and temporary reservists, large numbers of whom were over enlistment age. By May 1945, almost 17,000 WACs were serving in all overseas theaters and WAVES, SPARS, and Women Marines were serving in U.S. territories overseas. But the bulk of their members served in the continental United States. Women comprised 18 percent of naval shore personnel and 55 percent of the uniformed personnel in Navy Department Headquarters in Washington. So women comprised a significant proportion of personnel carrying out four continental duties: civilians producing armaments for all the Allies, military personnel releasing men for combat, military personnel supporting a vast logistical and communications network, and those serving the continental defense system.

Finally, in reading the wartime issues of *The New York Times*, the question arose, how is it that during the war women were so included in the news, but vanished from history after the war was over? Part of the answer lies in how military history is written in America. Usually, it consists of accounts of military strategies devised and battle tactics employed, written mostly by men. In Europe, however, a lateral view is taken. War is discussed in terms of how it relates to political, social, and economic conditions. Until war becomes described as an integrated operational system--of political factors; of economic mobilization; of social conditions; of technical, logistical, and medical support--women's roles will be diminished. The genius of the American military has always resided in its planning and organizational capabilities. Women have always played important roles in these areas.

* * * *

I would like to express my thanks to Dr. Linda Grant De Pauw and The MINERVA Center for publishing this book. For more than ten years, the Minerva Center has been the sole institutional beacon providing guidance for those of us studying women's military history. Not coming from an academic background, I know I would have had a harder time getting published elsewhere. Other publishers, however, do not have the influence The MINERVA Center does, or the visibility within the military community. My great thanks also go to John Eisenhower for writing his wonderful introduction. Eleanor Stoddard has been a superb editor. She crafted my words and supplied content suggestions. Through her own knowledge of war events, she also provided balance and perspective. Debra E. Morgenstern, our production editor, did a beautiful job on the copies and provided moral and logistical support as well. The members of the different armed services, particularly the Coast Guard, were encouraging and extremely helpful in supplying materials and answering questions. My particular thanks goes to the Army Nurse Corps Historian Mlajor C. J. Moore for her advice and a wonderful set of photographs. Without the work of the 50th Anniversary of World War II Commemoration Committee, many important facts would not have been available for publication. Finally, I must thank my friends and associates, Patricia Armstrong; Col. O. W. Martin, Jr., USA (Ret.), USCG-AUX; Ralph Groves; Petty Officer Dave Riley, USCG; Gary Hartman; and Dr. Kathleen Williams for their advice and help with research and production.

What I hope I achieved in this book is to make readers realize that there is more depth to and unresearched material on women's military history than has been assumed by most. If I have done that, there will be people who can track the trails from some of the markers I have left.

C. Kay Larson

Raft on which the Bell and Shaw families and crew members survivived for twenty days on the Atlantic. Photo taken by crew member of the British Navy destroyer at the time of the rescue.

1

A World at War

From the day Great Britain declared war on Nazi Germany, American women became involved in the conflict--first as victims, later as belligerents. On the night of September 3, 1939, a German submarine torpedoed and sank the British passenger liner, S.S. *Athenia*, with 1,103 passengers on board. Among the 112 dead were twenty-eight Americans. After that date, any Americans traveling in international waters ran the risk of having their ships attacked. Although passenger ships were supposedly off limits, the Germans were never totally discriminating. In May of 1941, the S.S. *Zam Zam*, a neutral Egyptian liner with 150 Americans on board, was sunk in the South Atlantic.[1]

Historically an intrepid group, American missionaries found their faith tested traveling in wartime. An unnamed missionary on her way to Africa had her ship sunk. She spent several months on a prison ship and more in a German camp. Released, she returned

1

to the United States and in October 1943 was in basic training with the Army Nurse Corps.[2]

Mrs. Ethel Bell, a widowed missionary, and her two children decided to leave the Vichy-controlled Ivory Coast in June of 1942. (The German army invaded France in the spring of 1940, but did not fully occupy it until November of 1942 when the Allies invaded North Africa. Prior to that time, a puppet government was installed at Vichy, France.) After traveling for one month to reach the British Gold Coast and another month in port, their ship, a cargo vessel containing palm oil, finally departed Takoradi for New York. On board was another missionary family, the Shaws with their three children, and a British customs agent. Otherwise, there were fifty American crew members.

On August 30, their ship was torpedoed and quickly sank, leaving only four eight-by-ten-foot rafts for survivors to get away in. Mrs. Bell, her children, two of the Shaw children, and fourteen crewmembers were cramped into one. Fortunately, they had an enterprising boatswain on board who jury-rigged a sail, and they set a course for Trinidad, immediately rationing their meager supply of food and water. During their twenty days at sea, sharks were their constant companions. Miraculously, their small craft failed to capsize during one storm which created 20-foot waves. Two men died on board. Mrs. Bell tried to keep spirits up and minds together by holding prayer meetings.

After two weeks, an American bomber sighted them and dropped food and water. The next day, however, the rescue ship which was sent failed to spot them. Finally, four days later, a merchant convoy accompanied by two naval destroyers, appeared. One destroyer broke off and headed toward the raft. Exultation, however, quickly turned to terror. "Then the incredible happened. Even as we watched, there was a roar and a leaping flame from her deck as a shell screamed over our heads, to hit the water a short distance behind us! It was quickly followed by another and another till [sic], with a sickening horror, we realized that we were being shelled!" The destroyer crew thought they had found a submarine.

The rafters quickly ripped down their mast and sail and began to wave it as a sign of truce. The firing stopped immediately, although by that time sixteen shots had landed quite near. Mrs.

Bell, et al., were taken aboard, medically treated, and transferred that afternoon to a Dutch ship en route to Barbados. After hospitalization, the Bells and others were flown to New York.[3]

American women also left the States to aid the war effort before the United States entered the war. As early as 1941, Red Cross nurses were making the crossing to England. By the summer more than sixty had arrived. Some were lucky to make it; others didn't. Seventeen nurses were on a Dutch ship that was sailing for the British in June 1941 when it was torpedoed. Two perished. In the same month, four Red Cross nurses and a Marine corporal were plucked from a lifeboat by a Navy destroyer which spotted them on July 5. Their torpedoed ship had sunk in six to eight minutes on June 24. They had subsisted for twelve days and eleven nights on rationed canned meatballs, hard tack, and water, including rainwater that they had collected in empty cans. Two of their fellow female shipmates endured seven more days with seven sailors whom they nursed (two died on board).[4]

American women doctors also volunteered. In October 1941, Dr. Barbara Stimson, niece of Secretary of War Henry L. Stimson and sister of Julia Stimson, former Army Nurse Corps superintendent, and Dr. Achsa Bean were working in London for the British Emergency Medical Service. Stimson was assigned to the Royal Free Hospital, which was a casualty clearing station. Through arrangements made with the Red Cross, eight other women doctors were to join them soon.[5]

Other civilians made their way to Europe. Mrs. Seton Porter of New York City departed for France in March 1940. She had organized a group called "Le Paquet au Front," which sent relief packages to soldiers manning the Maginot fortifications on the German border. When leaving, she told reporters she expected "to engage in relief work near the front."[6]

Probably the very first American Army nurses to make the dangerous trip did so in September 1941. This group arrived in Reykjavik, Iceland to work at the base hospital there. American troops had occupied the island in July at the request of its government. Four months later, Jane Goodell and thirteen other Red Cross recreation workers landed. An intelligence officer later told Goodell that their convoy had passed through a wolfpack of twelve German submarines on its eighth day out.[7]

American women living in Europe soon felt the impact of the war. A few joined the British women's services. Those in France became "targets of suspicion" while the United States was still neutral. Once America entered the war, they became enemy aliens and were required to register at town hall offices once a week. Then, in September of 1942, American women living in France were sent to prison at Vittel Spa in eastern France where British citizens were already interned. (Exemptions were given to elderly women and mothers with children.)

Not all American women sat by and watched the German war machine roll over Europe. In 1936, American-born Helen Gregory formed a Polish Women Sharpshooters Civilian Regiment in Jaslika, Poland at the suggestion of her brother-in-law, after she had been rejected by the Polish Women's Police Brigade. An army officer agreed to drill the first twenty-five recruits and the town eventually supplied guns and ammunition. Soon the idea spread and regiments formed across Poland. The women adopted a green uniform with the white Polish eagle on the buttons. Gregory visited the United State later, and when she tried to return in 1937, she was refused passage. So when Germany invaded Poland, Gregory was not there to lead her units. She knew, however, that the women had fought bravely and side by side with the men. "Some died...still others were captured. I received letters from some saying they are in 'convents.' That means they are in concentration camps." Sometimes she wished she'd been with women, but she said by being in America "maybe I can tell others what they stood for." After lecturing for the Red Cross and working in a Canadian defense factory, Gregory returned to the States and in late 1943, joined the Coast Guard and was doing radio work.

Virginia Hall, who later worked for the Office of Strategic Services (OSS), which was the forerunner of the Central Intelligence Agency, was working for the U.S. Department of State in Estonia at the outbreak of the war. She went to England and after being refused entrance into the Auxiliary Territorial Services (probably because of a leg amputation required as a result of a hunting accident in Turkey), she journeyed to Paris on her own and became a French army ambulance driver for an artillery unit on the Western front. Another future secret agent, Devereaux Rochester, became an ambulance driver for the American Hospital in Paris. Mrs. Max Dixon, whose husband was from Brooklyn, New York also drove an ambulance and worked in the Resistance. For her work, she was awarded the Croix de Guerre by the French Government. In May 1942, she was still in Paris with her children and was arrested by the Germans. At the time, her husband had been trying to get them home for months.[8] In June 1942, Ruth Mitchell of Milwaukee, sister of General Billy Mitchell of the Army Air Forces, was exchanged for a German prisoner in Lisbon. The previous year, while living in Belgrade, Yugoslavia, she had joined the "revolutionary death-scorning Comitajdi," a Serbian resistance group. She had been a member of the general staff and a dispatch rider for its leader.[9]

In the Far East, as the war clouds darkened, American, British, and other women were making similar decisions to stay or to return home. In December 1941, the troop transport, *Wakefield*, was diverted from Capetown, South Africa to Singapore to land troops. On January 30, it was attacked by Japanese bombers, but was able to make repairs and depart with five hundred women and children for Bombay. Singapore fell on February 15, and some remaining women were taken prisoner. Judith Harlan, who as a child lived in Niagara Falls, New York during the war, remembers her mother giving a party for one of her nursing class friends who had been evacuated from Singapore on such short notice that she left with only the clothes she was wearing. Says Harlan, "I remember my mother being dressed up and with tea sandwiches and candles on the dining room table. She had invited neighbors and classmates over to welcome the woman, who was still wearing the same dress which at least by this time had been laundered, and to give her donations of clothing."[10]

During the war, American nationals were held in camps in China, Hong Kong, Indonesia, Malaysia, the Philippines, Taiwan, and Vietnam. One of these was Charlotte Gower, formerly dean of women at Lingnan University in Hong Kong. She was interned in a Japanese camp and while in prison taught fellow inmates Chinese. Released in a prisoner exchange after five months, she returned to the United States and joined the Marine Corps Women's Reserve. She was promoted to the rank of captain and worked for the Office of Strategic Services in Washington, D.C.[11]

Prior to America's entry into the war, women at home were taking it upon themselves to repel invaders, true to a centuries-old tradition of female militia groups. Disturbed by accounts of German paratroop tactics in Belgium and the Netherlands, forty-nine members of the National Legion of Mothers of America met in Manhattan in May of 1940 to form an antiparatroop rifle corps, "in case any such thing should ever come our way." The acting regional director, Mrs. Edna Johnston, told the press that they planned to involve their two million members in active posts around the country. The Veterans of Foreign Wars was arranging target practice facilities for them and Lt. Arthur Lockwood, U.S. Naval Reserve, who attended the meeting, presented the group with two rifles for starters.

Johnston was clearly the driving force in this movement since the next month the Molly Pitcher Brigade, apparently a commemorative group of which she was also a member, announced the launching of a similar group. By July, units had formed, as Mrs. Virginia Brindle of Hillside, New Jersey, who had been drilling with a Newark "Brigade," told of plans to organize one in Union County. Although the women were focusing on rifle marksmanship training, they were also studying ambulance driving, first aid, and air raid and canteen work.[12]

By 1942, other women's home defense groups had formed in Illinois, Kansas, and New Hampshire. The Illinois group was composed of Northwestern University students. Aside from marksmanship and drilling, the women studied or trained in mass feeding, motor transport, auto mechanics, military intelligence, and nursing.[13]

The actions of these women may seem amusing to us now, but in 1942 they wouldn't have been. Military plans included those to counter the landing of enemy forces. Indeed, two groups of German saboteurs were deposited on Long Island and in Florida from submarines in June of 1942.[14]

2

Pearl Harbor

At 7:56 a.m., Sunday, December 7, 1941, Japanese torpedo bombers flew in over Pearl Harbor naval base at Honolulu, Hawaii, and dive bombers attacked the Army's Hickam Field nearby. Within two hours, they had crippled or sunk eighteen warships and destroyed or damaged 347 aircraft. The Pacific battleship fleet was basically annihilated. Aircraft at Hickam, which had been parked wingtip to wingtip as an antisabotage measure, were wiped out on the ground. A few Army fighters from Wheeler Field managed to take off and down several Japanese planes. More than four thousand army and airmen and sailors were killed or wounded. America was at war. [1]

One of the first persons to sight the incoming Japanese planes was Cornelia Fort, a flight instructor at John Rogers Airport on the island. She was up in her small plane with a student giving an early morning lesson to prepare him for his first solo flight. Suddenly they saw a military plane coming towards them, and Fort grabbed the controls and pulled up just in time to miss it. Then she recognized the red balls of the Japanese rising sun on the tops of the wings. She turned and looked at the harbor and saw clouds of black smoke rising. Still thinking, or hoping, that this was some kind of maneuver, she turned her gaze above her to see a bomber formation and watched one of their bombs fall. At that point, the full reality of the situation sank in, and as she told it, "I knew the air was not the place for my little baby airplane and I set about landing as quickly as ever I could. A few seconds later a shadow passed over me and simultaneously bullets spattered all around me." Fort would later become a member of the Women's Auxiliary Ferry Squadron (WAFS).[2]

Undoubtedly by the time Fort landed her plane, military nurses at local hospitals had already been inundated with casualties. In December 1941, the Army Nurse Corps consisted of seven thousand members, with eighty-two stationed at three medical facilities on Oahu.[3] Marie Conter was on duty that morning and recalled that she first became aware of the sound of the planes coming in low, and she thought one was going to crash. She went to look outside and saw a Japanese plane. Not believing the sight, she asked the patients, who couldn't believe it either, so Conter ran downstairs to the commanding officer. He just kept nodding in the affirmative, as he furiously dialed the phone. The staff was able to move the patients to the first floor as the attack progressed. As Conter wrote to her parents at the end of December, "'Well, the sight in our hospital I'll never forget. No arms, no legs, intestines hanging out, etc. . . . the hangars all around us were burning--and that awful 'noise.' Then comes the second attack--we all fell face down on the wounded in the halls, O.R., and everywhere and heard the bombers directly over us." The nurses in Conter's hospital slept there in uniform for a week, and officers' wives who were registered nurses helped for days.[4]

As the large numbers of wounded flowed in, hospital corridors were soon filled, with many men lying on the floors. Surgeons passed instruments back and forth between themselves at operating tables. Cleaning rags became face masks, and doctors and nurses operated without gloves. Besides the terrible loss-of-limb injuries, there were also severe burn cases because of the fires and explosions on the ships, and men came in coated with black oil.

For her work on that fateful day, First Lt. Annie G. Fox, chief nurse at Hickam Field, became the first nurse of World War II to be awarded a Purple Heart. This decoration was originally conferred on military men by Gen. George Washington during the American Revolution for "outstanding performance of duty and meritorious acts of extraordinary fidelity." Since 1932, however, the medal has usually been awarded for injuries received as a result of enemy action. Fox was not wounded but received the medal for her example of "calmness, courage and leadership, which was of great benefit to the morale of all she came in contact with."[5]

Navy medical units, which included a marine hospital, a mobile hospital, and two smaller treatment facilities, also received casualties that day. The newly commissioned hospital ship, U.S.S. *Solace*, was moored near battleship row when the attack began. Navy Nurse Anna Danyo was thrown out of her bunk by the force of the explosions. Within minutes, Chief Nurse Grace Lally was at her door telling her to report to the quarterdeck. Said Lally, "I had been in the battle zone in China . . . I realized what we thought couldn't happen was happening." The *Solace* crew soon found they had special reason to be concerned about their safety and that of their patients as the ship became caught in a crossfire between antiaircraft guns trying to shoot down Japanese planes. But, as one nurse put it, they, "didn't have time to be scared." During the day, the *Solace* took on 132 wounded.[6]

Over the course of the next four years, more than 59,000 women would serve in the Army Nurse Corps. Another 14,000 would serve in the Navy Nurse Corps. American nurses served in all theaters throughout the world--in England and through all the European campaigns, in Africa, China, Burma, India, Australia, New Zealand, New Guinea, Guadalcanal, New Caledonia, the Philippines, the Solomons and other islands in the Pacific, and on hospital ships. Among them were some five hundred black Army nurses. First Lt. Sue Freeman headed a group of thirty nurses at the 25th Station Hospital at Roberts Field in Liberia. First Lt. Agnes B. Glass was chief nurse at the 335th Station Hospital in Tagap, Burma.[7]

Florence Smith Finch looks on as Rear Adm. Howard Gehring, USCG and Capt. Dennis Egan, USCG unveil photo and plaques that will hang in the new Smith Building at Coast Guard Base Honolulu. SPAR Smith was a member of the Manila underground and joined the Coast Guard in mid-1945 after liberation from a Japanese internment camp. Honolulu, February 1995, U.S. Coast Guard, Commandant's Bulletin

3

The Philippines

In the early morning hours of December 8, 1941, Gen. Douglas MacArthur in Manila, the Philippines, was notified of the Japanese attack on Pearl Harbor and ordered his troops to take up battle stations. Clark Air Field, located northwest of the city, was hit hours later. At midday on December 10, the attack on Manila began, and Jean MacArthur and their small son, Arthur, watched it from the Manila Hotel penthouse. Within forty-eight hours, the core of American air power in the islands had been destroyed, and the U.S. fleet at Cavite Naval Base was crippled, leaving only land forces which had no way to be resupplied. Although the Americans and Filipinos put up a courageous resistance over the next five months, those first two days of the Japanese attack doomed them.[1]

As Japanese forces advanced south across the main island of Luzon and occupied territory, American citizens living in the areas were placed in camps around the island and remained imprisoned during the war. In 1945, the internees would be moved to Manila prisons as the Japanese retreated south in the face of invading American troops. Large numbers of women would number among the almost four thousand civilians liberated in February 1945. They would include civilian Army contract nurses, a former World War I physical therapist, and Red Cross personnel.

Also on Luzon at the time of the attack were eighty-eight Army nurses, three dietitians, and one physical therapist from the Medical Specialist Corps. They were mostly located at the Sternberg General Hospital in Manila and at Fort McKinley outside the city. Two nurses were stationed at Camp John Hay in the north. Thirteen nurses were located at Fort Mills on the island of Corregidor. The few nurses working at Fort Stotsenberg Station Hospital adjacent to Clark Field endured the three hour air attack on December 8, and were inundated with casualties.

As Japanese troops moved south towards Manila, nurses outside that city relocated to it. At the end of the month, MacArthur withdrew the bulk of his forces to the Bataan peninsula and made his headquarters on Corregidor. By December 25, one Navy and fifty-one Army nurses had been sent to Bataan to set up two hospitals. A front line one was established at Limay; an evacuation hospital was set up at Cabcabin. Conditions at both were primitive. On January 10, one former Army Nurse Corps member who would be recommissioned in 1945 joined the Cabcabin unit. At the end of the month, the Limay hospital was moved to Little Baguio, a jungle site on the Real River.

By December 29, twenty-one more nurses, the physical therapist, and one dietitian had evacuated Manila. Another nurse left with wounded for Australia on the hospital ship, *Mactan*. The two nurses stationed at Camp John Hay stayed to treat wounded there. They finally withdrew with the rest of the force, trekking thirty hours through the mountains. On December 28, they were captured at a civilian encampment to which they had made their way.

By January, most of the Navy nurses in the Far East had been taken prisoner. Five were taken on Guam on December 10, sent to prison in Japan and repatriated in Mozambique in August 1942, with members of the diplomatic corps. When the attack came on the Philippines, eleven Navy nurses were stationed at the Canacao Naval Hospital. After a bombing raid destroyed the hospital on December 11, they were sent to Manila where they established a hospital at the Santa Scholastica Musical College. These eleven were captured when Manila fell and would be imprisoned at the Santo Tomas Internment Camp until 1943. At that time, they left to set up a prisoner-of-war camp infirmary at Los Banos from which they were liberated in 1945. A twelfth Navy nurse, who had left with the Army group for Bataan, was evacuated from Corregidor in May with Army nurses, the only Navy nurse to escape.[2]

During this same time, Jean MacArthur and Arthur, had also been moved to Corregidor. On February 21, Mrs. MacArthur refused the chance to evacuate with the president of the Philippines and the American governor. The next day, General MacArthur received orders from President Franklin Roosevelt and Gen. George Marshall to leave for Australia to assume command of American forces. Reluctant to abandon his troops, MacArthur stayed until the night of March 11. Then he, Jean, Arthur, and seventeen staff members boarded four PT boats for a grueling six hundred mile trip through the Mindoro Strait.

Their first obstacle was the minefield off Corregidor. Having successfully slithered through it, at 9:15 p.m. the boats opened up to full throttle, which after months of wear meant a speed of only twenty-three knots (27 m.p.h.). At that rate, enemy destroyers could easily overtake them or aircraft could attack them. There was also a strong wind and waves of fifteen to twenty feet through which the boats pounded. Bonfires on shore indicated that they had been sighted by coastal watchers. The PTs became separated in the night, and it was later learned that one broke down. The other three managed to rendezvous off Cuyo Islands the next morning. One boat's hull was leaking, so the crew was switched to another. The party anchored for a few hours and then decided to leave, risking the daylight trip. During the next sixteen hours, the helmsmen managed to evade one Japanese cruiser, one destroyer, and the guns of a coastal battery. Everyone on board had been wet, cold, and seasick from the start of the voyage. At one point, MacArthur "lay on the mattress in the 41 boat's lower cockpit, deathly ill again, gritting his teeth as his wife again rubbed his hands. Whether he understood the meaning of the activity topside [i.e., evasion] is unknown, but Jean, though she was vomiting herself, heard everything and, a crewman said, "she didn't turn a hair."

After thirty-five hours at the helm, the 41's skipper put the boat in at the Del Monte plantation on Cagayan Island, exactly at the prearranged time of seven a.m. General MacArthur, now recovered from seasickness, helped his wife ashore. The party spent the next four days nervously awaiting B-17s from Australia. Japanese troops had been alerted to their presence and were moving to capture them. The flight to Australia was also eventful. There was turbulence, and pilots had to evade Japanese fighters looking for them, which produced airsickness. The plane was forced to land at an airport fifty miles from Darwin because that base was under attack. From there they flew on to Alice Springs. With Jean MacArthur now refusing to take another plane to Melbourne, the family boarded a rustic train complete with cowcatcher, for a 70-hour trip. When they reached Adelaide to switch to a luxurious private car supplied by the government, reporters met them and General MacArthur made his now famous pronouncement, "I came through and I shall return."[3]

Meanwhile, American and Filipino forces were still holding out on Bataan. By the end of March, "All medical installations on Bataan were bursting with [10,000] patients and still they were not able to care for all the sick and wounded." The hospital at Little Baguio was bombed twice. On March 30, it received a direct hit from bombs, killing over one hundred patients and strewing body parts everywhere, some hanging from tree branches. One nurse recalled, "The sergeant pulled me under the desk, but the desk was blown into the air, and he and I with it. I heard myself gasping. My eyes were being gouged out of their sockets, my whole body felt swollen and torn apart by the violent pressure. Then I fell back to the floor,and the desk landed on top of me and bounced around. The sergeant knocked it away from me, and gasping for breath, bruised and aching, sick from swallowing the smoke from the explosive, I dragged myself to my feet."

As the weeks passed, staff and patients began to suffer from malnutrition. This made them more subject to such tropical diseases as malaria, beri beri, and dysentery. One day before the surrender of Bataan, the medical personnel were evacuated to Corregidor Island. There the 500-bed Malinta Hospital was set up in a large tunnel, which eventually had to accommodate one thousand patients. The close, dirty quarters became thick with the stench of disinfectants, anesthetics, and "too many people." Incessant bombings raised the dust levels and loosened the tunnel walls. Often electricity was cut off. During this time two nurses were injured.

When commanding Gen. Jonathan Wainwright determined that he had no choice but to surrender the Philippines to the Japanese, he attempted to evacuate some of the nurses. Of the two Navy planes that left with twenty nurses each on April 29, only one reached Australia. The other had to make a forced landing on Lake Mindanao, and all were taken prisoner. Eleven other Army nurses, one Navy nurse, and the wife of a naval officer were picked up by a submarine on May 3, and taken to Australia. After Wainwright formally surrendered on May 6, the remaining fifty-five nurses and Medical Specialist Corps personnel were taken prisoner, along with the rest of the American troops. They would eventually be imprisoned at the Santo Tomas Internment Camp in Manila. In September 1943, one of the Camp John Hay nurses who had been imprisoned in the north joined them.[4]

During this same time, one young Filipino-American woman, Florence Ebersole Smith, had evaded Japanese authorities. Smith grew up in the Philippines, since her father had been an American army man who had gone there to fight in the Spanish-American War and stayed. Prior to the fall of Manila in January 1942, she worked for a Lieutenant Colonel Engelhart as a stenographer in the Army's Office of Military Intelligence, along with two other secretaries. While employed there, she met Charles Smith, a Navy PT boat crewman. They married in August 1941, and he was killed in February supplying Corregidor.

In June 1942, Smith began to work for the Manila underground. Unaware of her previous employment record, the Japanese hired her as an inventory clerk at the Philippine Liquid Fuel Distributing Union. Says Smith, "I was chosen for my neat handwriting." Vouchers for gasoline and other fuels were soon being neatly issued to the resistance. Smith also made arrangements for fuel supplies to be destroyed while being shipped.

After Wainwright's surrender, American troops were marched through the streets of Manila. Smith and the other secretaries watched their former boss go by and said she, "He and I made eye-to-eye contact." Shortly thereafter, she received a note from Engelhart asking her for soap and quinine for him and the other inmates imprisoned north of the city. The secretaries smuggled "everything we could to them" and even started a weekly laundry service for the men. Of this work, she said the people of Manila were "very loyal and eager to help." Living in Manila, Smith's work was particularly risky as she was more subject to "visits" by Japanese authorities. In spite of the danger, she continued her resistance work until October 1944[5]

Jean MacArthur and Arthur V at Del Monte Field, Mindanao, after PT boat ride from Corregidor, 13-14 March. 1942. MacArthur Memorial Archives, Norfolk, Va.

4

Wolves at the Door

Back in the United States, at the time of Pearl Harbor, President Franklin D. Roosevelt called the Congress into session and on December 8, 1941, declared war on Japan. Three days later, German Chancellor Adolf Hitler declared war on the United States.

On December 12, Hitler met with German Naval Chief Erich Raeder, and they decided to send submarines to raid commerce off eastern seaboard. This would become tantamount to a German Pearl Harbor in terms of its threat to the American mainland. Although action was delayed for one month, as of mid-January 1942, there were nineteen German U-boats operating in the United States strategic area. On January 12, the British passenger ship *Cyclops* became the first victim when it was sunk three hundred miles off Cape Cod, Massachusetts. During the month of February alone, 432,000 tons of shipping were sunk in the Atlantic, eighty percent of the total off the American coast. By May 14, officials estimated that 180 ships had been lost since the middle of January.

The problem for the Navy at this point was having to mobilize for a two-ocean war with German submarines at one doorstep. A critical shortage of warships existed. Naval leaders also failed to react quickly or effectively to meet the crisis. Chief of Naval Operations Ernest J. King would have preferred to fight the war in the Pacific first although the Americans and the British had previously decided that Europe would have priority. In 1942, talks about a European invasion were already underway, and King believed that in a few months the submarine threat would diminish. He disliked the British and initially rejected their advice to establish a coastal convoy system for merchant ships crossing the Atlantic, although one was implemented by May.

Ship captains were making the mistake of plying near-shore at night, which only succeeded in making their silhouettes perfect targets for surfaced U-boats. This was particularly true when coming out of East Coast ports, as these cities did not immediately dim their lights.

Admiral Adolphus Andrews was the officer charged with East Coast defense. At the beginning of April 1942, he had only sixty-five Coast Guard cutters, three 173-foot patrol craft, twelve Eagle boats and converted yachts, and fourteen armed British trawlers to deal with the threat. By June, more than 1,000 Coast Guard Auxiliary and other craft had been taken into service. To help them, Army, Navy, and Civil Air Patrol (CAP) planes were also flying antisubmarine patrols, as were blimps based in New Jersey.

During 1942 government officials were preparing for every contingency and trying desperately to deal with the submarines. As late as September, a Navy directive to patrol boats read:

> It may be assumed that enemy actions will take one of the following forms:
> (a)   Submarine activity against shipping
> (b)   Aircraft attack on New York vicinity
> (c)   Surface craft employed as raiders or scouts
> (d)   Attempts to land ground forces

(e)   The laying of mines in coastal waters by submarine, surface vessels, or aircraft

(f)   Bombardment of shore objectives by submarine or surface vessels.[1]

To meet the crisis, American women and girls, as well as men, were mobilized. In New York City women civilian defense volunteers helped issue more than 150,000 port security and vessel identification cards. In January, the Army was calling for fifty women a week to serve as plotters who would chart and trace all planes in the New York City area. By July, the need was such that thirty younger women, aged sixteen to eighteen, reported for this duty with the Aircraft Warning Center (AWC) of the 1st Fighter Command, and fifty more were being recruited from the Junior Auxiliary of the American Women's Voluntary Services, a civil defense group. The New York City civil defense office was appealing for four hundred women for the AWC to sign up immediately. These positions would eventually be filled by women in the Women's Army Auxiliary Corps. (WAAC)..[2]

Women also joined and assisted the Coast Guard Auxiliary. This volunteer civilian component of the Coast Guard was formed in 1939 to promote recreational boating safety and to assist the Coast Guard in search and rescue. Private boat owners used their own vessels and were specially trained by their members and supervised by the Coast Guard. Throughout the country many of these units began 24-hour port security patrols the night of December 7 and on December 8. They also served as seamanship training units for men and women going into the naval forces. As merchant ships were torpedoed off the Atlantic Coast and in the Gulf of Mexico, these Auxiliarists took out their tiny boats, sometimes only armed with rifles, to rescue the crews. Members serving with the Coastal Picket Force did antisubmarine duty and could find themselves depth-charging U-boats.

Today, many wives of male Auxiliarists serve as unofficial members, helping with meetings, social events, and recruiting. Wives appear to have assisted in like manner during the war. Women were always eligible to become members, but it is not known exactly when the first women joined. Betty McNabb, later

19

a renowned auxiliary and CAP pilot, recalled first joining the Auxiliary in 1941 when her unit was run by her parents in Florida. By 1943, there were approximately one hundred women members, mostly located in the Lake Winnebago area of Wisconsin. Many of these women owned their own boats and were active in training and public education. A number were in training for commissions in the Navy and Coast Guard. In the 11th Naval District in California an all-female flotilla was also being organized.

Auxiliarist Jean Linderman carried out one of the more unusual duties for a woman during the war. She lived in Florida, owned her own boat and was qualified as a boatswain's mate second class. She also owned and lived on her own Florida Key, Liar's Lair. Because it was considered too time-consuming and expensive to teach men what she already knew and to house them on her key, she was allowed to conduct her own exclusive boat patrols in "one whole section of the keys."[3]

In New Jersey, state civil air defense pilots were flying "routine observation" (read antisubmarine) patrols for the Army and Navy. They also ferried planes and served as couriers. As of February 1942, fifteen percent of the five hundred air defense members were women. Ruth Cheney Streeter was one of the pilots. To her disappointment, she was later assigned as adjutant of Group 221, Civil Air Patrol, and others flew her plane. She would later become director of the Marine Corps Women's Reserve and encourage Women Marines to fill aviation slots.

Cecil "Teddy" Kenyon was another woman who conducted antisubmarine patrols with the civil air patrol in the New York region. Appropriately, she was a descendant of Alexander Hamilton, father of the Coast Guard. It is not clear whether Kenyon flew with a state unit or sneaked in flights with the federal Civil Air Patrol. She went on to become a production test pilot for Grumman Aircraft Corporation on Long Island.[4] Early in the war, the New Jersey unit was absorbed into the federal Civil Air Patrol (CAP) in which women were prohibited from flying patrols. Even so, there was one CAP woman pilot who was an antisubmarine patrol instructor at a base in Florida. She was Dolly Heberding, who tried to convince her superiors that she could do a better job if she actually got to fly a patrol, but they did not accept her reasoning. She ultimately left to ground test Hellcat Dive Bombers.[5]

In July 1942, an integrated coastal patrol system was established by the Army, Navy, and Coast Guard. This consisted of foot, mounted, and canine patrols on the beaches, as well as inshore boat patrols. Extra watch towers and telephone jacks were added to the existing network of life-saving stations and lighthouses. At that time, one woman lighthouse keeper remained in the Coast Guard-- Fanny Salter of Turkey Point Light on the Chesapeake Bay in Maryland. She was a veteran of twenty years' service. Besides maintaining her light, Salter kept a radio watch and was responsible for reporting buoys that were "off station" or not working. Photographic evidence suggests that at least two other women helped the beach patrol personnel--one officer's wife perhaps as a riding instructor.[6]

As these members of the "home guard" were trying to protect shipping, some women merchant mariners were hoping they wouldn't be torpedoed. Immediately after Pearl Harbor, the government "beached" women members of the maritime union who served as radio operators, stewardesses, ship nurses, and waitresses. When the order went out, however, some were still at sea. As one described it, "We were four days out of New York when war was declared....We girls got out and painted the ship for camouflage and stood watch besides our regular routine." The women appealed the restrictive ruling, which to this author's knowledge was never totally lifted. One woman who urged a reversal was Mrs. Annie Russell, a mariner in World War I whose ship had been torpedoed.

Some women evaded the "beaching." In October 1943, Mary Hanisco and Alice Kimmerley signed on with Norwegian ships which were exiled in New York City and shipping war materiel. Their first voyage was to the Belgian Congo. Upon their return, Hanisco reported to the press that the only incident was the sighting of an enemy aircraft carrier and the ship changed course. En route home, Kimmerley took gunnery lessons. Hanisco contracted malaria and was recovering at a seaman's center in New Jersey. Ultimately, seventeen other American women mariners sailed with the Norwegian crews who also had their women on board.

The government prohibition on women mariners apparently did not apply to passenger liners. In March of 1944, Mrs. Edna Johansson of New Orleans, a former stewardess on the American liner *Sixoala* was awarded the War Shipping Administration combat bar with star. In June 1942, the *Sixoala* had been torpedoed near the Panama Canal. The star decoration was awarded only to persons who had had to abandon ship because of enemy actions.[7]

5

Axis Passions
Allied Victories

With America now at war, probably no officials in the United States knew that a resourceful Midwestern woman had been working for British intelligence for several years in Europe and had switched her operations to Washington after the fall of France. Code-named CYNTHIA, Amy Elizabeth Thorpe was the daughter of a Marine Corps major. Her mother came from a Minnesota political family. She had married a British diplomat who was stationed in Warsaw when she came to the notice of British intelligence officers in 1937. Bored with her often ill, absent, and dull husband, Thorpe was young, dynamic, good-looking, and found that men in diplomatic circles were attracted to her. She proceeded to use her charms for the benefit of the Allied cause, ultimately succeeding in a stunning espionage career.

One of Thorpe's first prewar conquests was the confidential aide to the Polish Foreign Minister Jozef Beck, who was on good terms with Berlin. She talked the aide into taking documents from Beck's office to be copied, and she went on trips to Berlin and Prague with him. Through him she gathered intelligence on the German cipher machine Enigma. Additional information she collected combined with that from other sources enabled the British, through the use of their ULTRA system, to read German message traffic throughout the war. (In encoding, words are substituted and in encrypting ciphers, i.e., letters or numbers are substituted randomly to make writing secret.)

Thorpe's activities in Poland began to attract attention, and because she was fluent in Spanish, as well as German and French, she was sent to Latin America to obtain information on pro-Nazi sympathizers and agents there. Then in 1940, the British needed someone to "work" French and Italian diplomats in Washington, so they set Thorpe up as a free-lance reporter with a house in Georgetown. There her first passionate victim was an Italian admiral she had known before the war and whom she, incredibly, persuaded to turn over the Italian naval code and cipher books for microfilming.

This intelligence coup reached fruition in the Mediterranean in March 1941, when Admiral Cunningham, forewarned of an Italian naval assault on British troop transports en route to Greece, moved to attack. In the resulting Battle of Cape Matapan, the British navy destroyed the Italian cruisers, *Pola, Fiume,* and *Zara* and damaged the battleship, *Vittorio Veneto.* Winston Churchill stated that these actions "disposed of all challenge to the British naval mastery in the Eastern Mediterranean at this critical time."

In May 1941, Thorpe was paid a personal visit by William Stephenson, head of the British Secret Intelligence Service. He wanted her to concentrate on two efforts--the Vichy navy and French funding of Nazi activities in the Americas. From this meeting, she went on to seduce one Charles Brousse, a former French naval pilot, then press secretary for the Vichy embassy in Washington. Brousse began to supply her with plain language copies of telegrams sent by and to the embassy and then daily reports on its events. One assessment of the importance of these documents reads, "The plain text undoubtedly enabled the British to reconstruct French diplomatic codes, if they had not already done so."

The other job Stephenson assigned Thorpe, the theft of the Vichy naval codes and ciphers, was the most important. By this time, Brousse was so implicated in her activities that he had no choice but to assist. Using the excuse of needing a place for love trysts, Brousse talked the security guard in the embassy into letting them have the use of a couch at night in one of the rooms. In the meantime, British Intelligence had secured the services of a Canadian safecracker who had been given early prison release to do secret service work. The plan was for Thorpe and Brousse to drug the guard while they let the Cracker into the code room to do his work. The first night, it took the Cracker until dawn to get the safe open because it was old. Since it was too late to photocopy papers, he wrote down the combination and gave it to Thorpe. Even with a tutoring lesson, Thorpe made two more attempts to open the safe, but failed. They decided to make one more try and bring in the safecracker again. On this final night, the guard stumbled upon the couple naked on the couch and fled in embarrassment. Thorpe had begun throwing off her clothes and demanding Brousse do the same when she heard the guard approach. With this diversion, the Cracker cracked the safe, the papers were smuggled out to an agent standing by, were copied and couriered to England.

Once the Vichy codes were supplied, the intelligence group at Bletchley Park in England could compare clear French messages with encrypted German traffic and hopefully speed the decrypting process. Information could possibly be gleaned on Nazi plans to take over French naval bases in North Africa or for an invasion of Spain, as well as on the remaining Vichy fleet at Toulon, Casablanca, and Alexandria. Finally, as Stephenson's biographer has written, "What CYNTHIA could not be told was that the ciphers seemed essential for the success of the plan for clearing North Africa of Axis forces in preparation for the assault on Europe." British reports credited Thorpe by stating, "A woman agent under the direction of B[ritish] S[ecurity] C[oordination] in

New York accomplished the most important work that opened the way back into France and ultimately into Germany." And so in November 1942, the long-awaited second front opened with the Allied invasion along the North African coast. Although Thorpe's work may seem less daring as she was living in her own country, with America still neutral and British Intelligence activities in the country a secret, she operated without official protection and at any time could have been targeted for assassination by the Germans.[1]

6

Mobilization

As the nation geared up to fight a war worldwide, men and industry were being mobilized, and attention turned to the women, too. During the first year of the war, bills were introduced into Congress to allow women to volunteer for service in the armed forces in capacities other than nurses. During World War I, the Navy and Coast Guard enlisted some 12,500 "Yeomen (F)," popularly known as "yeomanettes," for clerical and other duties, and the Marine Corps enrolled three hundred women clerks by the end of the war, but disbanded the units afterward. The Army recruited civilian telephone operators and clerks serving with the American Expeditionary Forces in Europe, under contract with the government.[1]

Although plans for future enlistment of women had been submitted to the War Department in the late 1920s, they gathered dust in file drawers. In January 1942, when Congresswoman Edith

Nourse Rogers submitted her second bill to form a Women's Army Auxiliary Corps (WAAC), support from officers like Gen. George Marshall, Army Chief of Staff, helped overcome Congressional opposition. The bill was signed into law by President Roosevelt on May 15, 1942, stipulating a ceiling of 150,000 members.

As members of an auxiliary corps, the women were not at first entitled to the same pay, benefits, protections, or titles as the men nor were they governed by Army regulation or the Articles of War. In July 1943 a new law was passed which integrated women into the Army of the United States with limitations on highest ranks. One rank of colonel was given to the director; other officers could not rise above lieutenant colonel. Those aged twenty to fifty could now join, as compared with twenty-one to forty-five previously. Enlisted personnel had to have completed two years of high school; officers needed two years of college training. The new name of the organization was the Women's Army Corps (WAC).[2]

The Navy legislation for women followed that of the Army and became law on July 30, 1942. It established a Women's Naval Reserve which was given the acronym, Women Accepted for Volunteer Emergency Service (WAVES). The Marine Corps Women's Reserve (MCWR) was established in the WAVES legislation. In November 1942, legislation establishing the Coast Guard Women's Reserve was passed. Its acronym, SPARs, stood for the Coast Guard motto, *"semper paratus*, always ready."* Legislation in June had authorized the enrollment of women temporary Reservists. The stated goal of all three Reserves was to have women release men for sea duty. WAACs had equal pay very soon. Because the naval women were assigned in ranks and ratings corresponding to those of the men, they received equal pay. The bulk of the women in the three services held support positions in the United States, although as of October 1944, the women were permitted to serve in Hawaii, Alaska, and locations in the American theater, which included all of North and South America.[3]

Like the Army, the highest rank of the directors of the naval reserves was established by law. By 1944, it had been changed to grant the WAVE and SPAR directors the rank of captain; the Women Marines' director was promoted to the equivalent rank of colonel. In the Navy and Marine Corps, women aged twenty to forty-nine could enroll. The age limit in the SPARs was fifty. All three naval services required enlisted personnel to have completed two years of high school. Officers had to either be college graduates or to have completed two years of college and have two years of acceptable work experience.[4]

The only Navy women to go to sea were Navy nurses on board hospital ships; they also trained medical corpsmen for duty on combat ships. In the Coast Guard only the rating of surfman allowed women on the water, as small boat instructors. SPAR radio operators handled distress, security, and operations message traffic from ships at sea.[5]

Even though they had been in existence since the beginning of the century, the Army and Navy Nurse Corps assigned only relative ranks to their members. The result was that members did not receive pay or benefits equal to men with corresponding duties.[6]

During the war, the directors of all the women's services wrestled with difficult policy questions regarding marriage, husbands and families, benefits, pregnancy, and fraternization to name a few. Changes in the laws and regulations that resulted are beyond the scope of this book.

By 1943, all the women's military services had been established. Hence, they came into competition with one another for volunteers, although they cooperated in local recruitment campaigns. It seems only the Women Marines easily met and surpassed their recruitment goal of 18,000 ahead of the target date. This success has been linked to the Marine Corps' reputation of being "the toughest, the bravest, the most selective."[7]

By the end of World War II, some 150,000 American women had served as WACs; 100,000 as WAVES; 23,000 as Women Marines; and 11,000 as SPARs, for a total of 284,000. The two nurse corps added another 73,000 women.[8]

Native American nurse cadets at the Ganado Mission in Arizona.
Presbyterian Church (U.S.A.), Department of History and
Records Management Services, Philadelphia, Pa.

WAACs Ruth Wade and Lucille Mayo work on service trucks,
Fort Huachuca, Az., December 8, 1942

7
Minority Women

The military services showed a mixed record in regard to the recruitment and training of minority women. The first WAAC Officer Candidate School class of 440 women included forty black women. Although segregated when the class opened in July 1942, the officer candidates were desegregated in November as a result of pressure from the National Association for the Advancementof Colored People and other groups. Black enlisted women, however, continued to be segregated in basic training and assigned to segregated units, usually with black officers. Black and white women did receive the same training and were assigned to the same military occupational specialties (MOS), and because of the small size of the specialized training units, these were desegregated.[1]

African-American women also served in aviation slots and were posted to ten airfields. At Douglas Army Airfield, they worked as aircraft mechanics and on the flight line. Black nurses were assigned to Tuskegee Air Field, serving the Tuskegee Fliers, the famous black pilot group. Janet Harmon, a black licensed pilot who owned her own plane and was a licensed nurse besides, became a final selectee for the Women Air Force Service Pilots (WASPs). However, Jacqueline Cochran, the director, persuaded her to withdraw her application since she felt that by adding race to the women's issue, the program as a whole could be jeopardized. Later Harmon tried to volunteer as a nurse, but was told the quota for black nurses was filled.[2]

For the first two years of the war, the Army Nurse Corps imposed a quota system on black nurses on the grounds that the women could treat only black patients. Due to political pressure the quota was lifted in 1944. Two thousand students then enrolled in the Cadet Nurse Corps, a Public Health Service training program, and black nursing schools received increased federal funding. In September 1945, however, there were only 479 black nurses in a corps of 50,000.

In January 1945, the Navy Nurse Corps lifted its color ban. In March, Phyllis Mae Daly of New York City, was the first to be commissioned. Only three others would enroll.[3]

In October 1944, a directive was issued requiring the Navy, Coast Guard, and Marines to begin enrolling black women on a non-discriminatory basis. In November, two cadets were admitted to the last training class for WAVE officers. One of them, Harriet Ida Pickens, graduated third in the class. Within six months seventy-two black enlisted women entered basic training. Six nurses became commissioned officers in the Navy Nurse Corps. A small number of black enlistees were accepted in the Coast Guard. The Marine Corps Women's Reserve did not enroll black applicants until 1949.[4]

Women from other minority groups also served, on a nonsegregated basis. Carmen Contreras-Bozak was the first Hispanic WAC member and Sergeant Vicenta R. Torres was one of the first to see duty in Italy. Many Puerto Rican WACs served in transportation commands, carrying out troop embarkment and disembarkment duties, among others. When Guatemala declared war on the Axis countries, Bertita Paniagua, daughter of a former Guatemalan diplomat, joined the Coast Guard.[5]

In early 1942, representatives of the Mohawk, Oneida, Seneca, Cayuga, Onondaga, Tuscarora, Chippewa, Sioux, and Navajo tribes met at a special convention and declared war on the Axis countries.

Approximately eight hundred Native American women enlisted in the WACs, WAVES, Women Marines, and the Army Nurse Corps. One entered the WASP program.

The major source of Native American recruitment was the Sage Memorial Hospital in Ganado, Arizona. It had the only accredited nursing school dedicated to the training of Native American nurses. The women represented more than fifty tribes. Over one-third of its total graduates entered the armed forces nurse corps, founded in 1930.

Dorothy Keating, who joined the WAVES in 1944, and trained as a pharmacist's mate, was a full-blooded Oneida from Wisconsin. Having been raised as a tomboy with four brothers (all of whom were in the service), she loved and excelled at the physical training since she had taken gymnastics as a teenager. It somewhat irritated her that her skills were attributed to the fact that she was a Native American. "Of course she could do it, because she's an Indian--like Indians were supposed to be very agile." Minnie Spotted-Wolf, a Blackfoot from Montana, was the first Native American to join the Women Marines.[6]

During the war, more than forty-five thousand Asian-Americans--those of Japanese, Chinese, Korean, and Filipino descent--joined the armed services. The exact number of women is unknown. Nisei women who were bilingual were sought as translators, working in intelligence and communications. In November 1944, forty-seven Nisei WACs and one Chinese WAC entered the Army's Military Intelligence School at Fort Snelling, Minnesota. They received the same training as the men but specialized in written language translation, as opposed to interrogation and oral translation which were more suited to assignment in the Pacific. Some nisei, however, were among the 150 WACs assigned to the Allied Translator and Intelligence Service in the Southwest Pacific where they served as translators and interrogators. In April 1945, three nisei were commissioned in the Army Nurse Corps. Two Chinese-American women were WASP members.[7]

Teresa Alvarez, railroad yard blacksmith's helper. AP/Wide
World Photos

Members of the WAC 6888th Postal Battalion sorting mail in
England, 1945. U.S. Army, WAC Museum, Ft. McClellan, Ala.

8

The Directors

The women appointed to serve as the leaders of the women's services had had distinguished careers prior to the war. Oveta Culp Hobby, director of the Women's Army Corps, 1942-1945, was the wife of a former governor of Texas, a former parliamentarian of the Texas house of representatives, a mother of two, a radio and newspaper executive, lawyer, and civic activist. She had also headed the women's interest section in the War Department's Bureau of Public Relations and had helped in planning for the WAAC. Hobby later served as Secretary of the Department of Health, Education, and Welfare during the Eisenhower Administration (1953-1955). She would also become an editor, president and chairman of the board of the *Houston Post*, and a member of numerous corporate boards and public interest groups. She was awarded the Distinguished Service Medal for her wartime service.[1]

The Army Nurse Corps (ANC) expanded notably under the leadership of Col. Florence A. Blanchfield. In June 1943, she took over as superintendent of nurses from Col. Julia Flikke. Blanchfield had held the position of personnel officer and in February 1939, had become assistant superintendent of the ANC. She was born in West Virginia, graduated from nurses' training schools in Pittsburgh, Pennsylvania and Baltimore, Maryland. Before World War I, she advanced to the position of superintendent of nurses at the Suburban General Hospital in Bellevue, Pennsylvania.

In April 1917, Blanchfield was given the relative rank of first lieutenant in the Army Nurse Corps and served as chief nurse for the American Expeditionary Forces in France. After demobilization in 1920, she rejoined the Corps and served in ten different positions in the United States, the Philippines, and China. During World War II, Blanchfield became known as "the soldiers' nurse," developing new care concepts which brought nurses closer to the front lines so that G.I.s would get nursing treatment sooner. She was instrumental in the passage of post war legislation that granted permanent commissions to nurses.

Capt. Sue S. Dauser, became the fifth superintendent of the Navy Nurse Corps in 1939 and was promoted to captain in 1942, serving throughout the war. The Navy nurses served on more than twelve hospital ships and in Navy hospitals throughout the world and across the nation.[2]

Mildred McAfee, head of the WAVES, was a Phi Beta Kappa graduate of Vassar College at age twenty, with a double major in economics and English. She had also been class president and a letter athlete. During the next fourteen years, she taught high school and college, served as executive secretary of the Vassar alumnae association, and earned a master's degree. In 1934, she was appointed dean of women at Oberlin College. Then in 1936, at age thirty-six, she became president of Wellesley College. She took a leave of absence to head the WAVES and moved up to the rank of captain.. After the war, having married Reverend Douglas Horton, she resumed the Wellesley presidency until 1949. She later became president of the American Association of Colleges and the National Social Welfare Assembly, vice president of the National Council of Churches and in 1962 was a delegate to the United Nations

Educational, Scientific, and Cultural Organization (UNESCO) General Conference. She also served on several boards of corporations.[3]

Dr. Dorothy Stratton, head of the Coast Guard SPARs, took a leave of absence from her job as dean of women at Purdue University. Born in Missouri, she graduated from Ottawa University in Kansas. She then alternated between teaching high school and studying for a Master's degree in psychology from the University of Chicago and a Ph.D. in philosophy from Columbia University. Stratton joined the Purdue faculty in 1933 and became a full professor of psychology in 1940. When the war broke out, she was one of a group of talented women educators who joined the military. She initially was commissioned as a lieutenant in the WAVES. Transferring into the Coast Guard, she became the first woman accepted for service in the Coast Guard Women's Reserve. After the war Stratton became the director of personnel for the International Monetary Fund and executive director of the Girl Scouts. She was the author of two books and a member of academic and professional societies.[4]

Ruth Cheney Streeter, director of the Marine Corps Women's Reserve, was the last service head to assume her post. In February 1943, she became the leader of a group that would train and use 23,000 women in Marine Corps jobs. She was awarded the Legion of Merit for her wartime service. She graduated from Bryn Mawr College in 1918, married, and was the mother of three sons in the service and one daughter. Aside from a long-standing interest in aviation and her work with the New Jersey civil air defense, she had been active in the New Jersey Relief Council and the New Jersey Commission on Interstate Cooperation. Later, she was a delegate to the New Jersey Constitutional Convention and a member of the Veterans' Service Council.[5]

Leadership and executive skills of the members of the directors' staffs contributed to their success. They brought backgrounds, in government, health, and education, which added depth to the organizations' expertise. Lt. Col. Mary-Agnes Brown, WAC staff director in the Southwest Pacific, had had Army experience in World War I in finance and later as an executive secretary and lawyer in the Veterans' Administration. She held

A.B., L.L.B. and S.J.D. degrees. Before assuming the position in the Pacific, she had been Hobby's executive officer.

Helen O'Neill also brought valuable military experience to her service. Prior to World War I, O'Neill had worked as a civilian employee in Navy headquarters. She enlisted and was quickly made a Chief Yeoman. After demobilization and for the next twenty years, O'Neill served as private secretary to many high ranking naval officials. When the Marine Corps Women's Reserve was created, she was directly commissioned a captain and served as Streeter's assistant.[6]

Leaders in the naval services were able to draw on the experience of an outstanding Women's Advisory Council headed by Dean Virginia Gildersleeve of Barnard College. These women had had many years' experience in administering women's programs at some of the best colleges and universities in the country. One early member, Dr. Lillian Gilbreth, was a management efficiency expert and mother of twelve.[7]

The leadership and executive skills of the women service directors and their staffs cannot be overemphasized. In scarcely more than one year, the WAAC organization grew to 60,243, and members were filling 155 Army jobs from the four originally authorized. In six months, the Army Nurse Corps expanded by ten thousand members. By January 1943, the WAVES had trained three classes of officers and had plans to open the U.S. Naval Training Station (Women's Reserve) in Bronx, New York. Recruitment had begun for SPAR and Women Marine officers.[8]

In a short period, training facilities were identified and set up, positions were defined and identified at bases all over the country, training curriculums were adapted, policy and regulations were formulated, uniforms were designed and made available, and officers and enlistees were on duty. At all times, the directors of the services were working in highly visible and politically sensitive positions, in uncharted territory. They also experienced the personal pressure of being national examples of female patriotism and propriety. Ruth Streeter pointed out that this was part of the rationale for establishing the director positions: "parents were not going to let their little darlings go in among all those wolves unless they thought that somebody was keeping a motherly eye on them."[9]

9

G.I. Janes

Five-thirty a.m. reveilles the first day of basic training convinced most women they were in the military. Tightly scheduled days filled with classes and physical training were the norm at the enlisted and officers' training schools. The women also received immunization shots to prevent disease; performed K.[itchen] P.[olice] duties; endured personal, room, and unit inspections; took tests; stood guard; and waited on long lines for the bathroom, meals, and ironing boards.

The Army was the first to open a training school, the First WAAC Training Center at Fort Des Moines, Iowa. The initial officer recruits arrived on July 20, 1942, and enlistes followed. Other schools were established in Florida, Georgia, Louisiana, and Massachusetts. The first class of officer candidates entered the Navy Midshipmen Training School at Smith College, Northampton, Massachusetts, in August. That fall, enlisted yeoman, storekeeper, and radio specialist schools opened. In

February 1943, the U.S. Naval Training Center (Women's Reserve) at Hunter College in the Bronx received WAVE, SPAR, and Women Marine recruits. Coast Guard and Women Marine officer candidates initially shared the Navy's Smith College center, which expanded to include facilities at Mount Holyoke College. By the summer of 1943, however, the Coast Guard was training enlisted personnel at its own facility in Palm Beach, Florida and later at its Manhattan Beach center in Brooklyn. Officer cadets went to the Coast Guard Academy at New London, Connecticut. At the same time, the Marine Corps set up enlisted and officer training at Camp LeJeune, North Carolina.[1]

Former WAVE Marilyn Willis recalls her parents' reaction to basic training. When she told them she had to clean the bathroom that twelve girls used, "My mother was appalled. 'What, my daughter should be cleaning toilets?' She didn't think I was fighting for my country by cleaning toilets. But, overall my parents were very supportive. My father just reminded me before I went in that if I didn't like it, I couldn't leave." Willis was rated as a yeoman and assigned to Navy Headquarters in Washington. She worked in the Bureau of Ships, which supplied advance bases in the Pacific.[2]

Classroom curriculums covered basic military topics and emphasized each service's specialties. Enlisted and officers learned military customs and courtesies, ranks and ratings, the organization and history of their services, regulations, procedures and first aid. Officers were taught leadership, command, public speaking, administration, military law and safeguarding information. Naval women digested nautical terminology and how to identify ships and aircraft. Women Marines learned about amphibious landing operations and tactics. Army women read maps and naval women read charts and swabbed decks.[3]

Because of the need to quickly utilize the women, officers and enlisted, who had civilian or military experience that was directly related to their duties or who needed no further training, were assigned to positions after graduating from basic training. Some went on to specialist schools. Naval officers were trained in finance, supply, communications, law, and other areas. Enlisted personnel were shipped to schools which trained them in aviation, technical, food preparation, radio, supply, medical, and transportation ratings. In all the services, the number of specialties in which the women qualified vastly increased during their service.[4]

The physical training the women received in basic training varied. Most recruits had to do calisthenics and marching. Navy schedules called for four hours of athletics or drilling every day. Coast Guard officer cadets found themselves rowing in small boats on the Thames River in New London, Connecticut. One finally complained to an instructor about her blister, "'Look,' I said pathetically, 'If I keep hauling on this chain, I'll get lockjaw.' He regarded me coldly. 'Lockjaw!,' he growled with a leer, 'What do you think you've had all those tetanus shots for? Haul away!'"[5]

The Women Marines had some of the toughest physical training. Marine Corps policy was to have the women receive instruction and exercise "similar to that of the men." Jean Horsfall of Massachusetts enlisted in 1943, and was athletic and physically fit at the time. She found the physical training, which included an obstacle course, very strict. The Marine drill instructors were too. Says Horsfall, "Our sergeants were straight from combat in the Pacific and were very tough on us. But when you got through your six weeks of basic training, you felt like a million dollars." While in basic training, public affairs people found out that Horsfall was an accomplished horsewoman. They found her a mount and she became the subject of a photo shoot. (She has no knowledge of what was done with the photographs.)[6]

The potential dangers of overseas duty were taken seriously by all the services. Former WAVE Marilyn Willis recalls that all recruits had to be able to swim forty yards in order to get away from a torpedoed ship. Women Marines embarked for Hawaii in 1944. Prior to leaving San Diego, they underwent more physical training. This included climbing up and down cargo nets with their packs on and jumping off ships into the water. WACs sent overseas also had special fitness training, namely, "judo, hikes with full packs, and an obstacle course which, although not required for noncombatants, every woman elected to go through." Interestingly, the women were also issued pistol belts with no pistols.[7]

The women whom the Army made sure were physically fit, and prepared for combat were the nurses. The first nurses sent overseas received no special training. Beginning in July 1943, however, all nurse recruits were required to go through four weeks of training which included Army medical and staff procedures and regulations. For physical training, they went on 20-mile marches with 30-pound packs. They also crawled through a 75-yard infiltration course which was laced with barbed wire. They learned to keep their heads low so as not to come in contact with the live machine gun bullets which zinged over their heads. Dynamite was exploded for added effect. When the *The New York Times* reported on the training in October, no nurse had yet "frozen" while going through.[8]

Among the reasons for the success of the women were the high quality and education levels of the volunteers. Aside from the physical requirements of height, weight, and vision, WAC members had to have police checks and employment and character references. As of July 1943, ninety-four percent of SPAR officers had college degrees and 20 percent had graduate degrees. Technical training in engineering, astronomy, metallurgy, statistics, physics, languages and other subjects were listed as "especially desired" skills for WAVES recruits. As an example, in December of 1940, there were only twelve men in the Navy fluent in written and spoken Japanese, so a training program was begun. The trainees had to either have had previous Japanese language training or be Phi Beta Kappa college graduates. There was soon a shortage of qualified men and the training was opened to women. In mid-1943, eighty-eight were selected according to the same criteria. They went to work in communications units in Washington. In another example, WAC mail censors in the Pacific handled all foreign, as well as all English mail. This required knowledge of thirty-one languages.[9]

The majority of women in all the services served in traditional female administrative and support positions. They became clerks, typists, stenographers, telephone and teletype operators, secretaries, postal clerks, and mail censors. One should not underestimate the importance of these positions, however, and they took on a particular wartime flavor. Government runs on paper, and those who are proficient in completing paperwork accurately and moving it quickly will move the military. Without the proper paperwork, there couldn't have been a war. Typing errors could have resulted in the wrong-sized shells being shipped with the wrong guns, in troops arriving and departing at incorrect times to wrong places, in flight plans going awry. The amount of paperwork and orders required to implement the D Day invasion, which sent tens of thousands of men on 5,000 ships off to France, is mind-boggling. Much of the clerical work was done by women working in difficult and dangerous conditions.[10]

The women's jobs could also be stressful. Signal Corps WACs were found to suffer from fatigue, depression, and mental breakdowns. A Mediterranean Theater inspector concluded that this was due to the "long hours over a period of several months under pressure caused by the necessity for speed and security in handling messages." Or, as another described the strain "one slip wrecked everything, and the fear of costing men's lives was always with them." The constantly rotating sleep schedules also wore down constitutions.[11]

Once Gen. Dwight Eisenhower brought WAACs to North Africa and their efficiency came to be seen, requests for them increased. In Europe, in the months prior to D Day:

> The War Department noted that, to meet the [European] theater's heavy demands for skilled typists and stenographers, not only would the entire recruiting intake be required, but it would be necessary for stations in the United States to resort to the embarrassing expedient of using male typists to replace Wacs 'for combat' instead of vice versa. The theater in reply urged that they be so embarrassed. In its opinion, overseas areas, being obliged to support and supply troops under difficulties, required the best workers for each type of duty; the argument was that one Wac typist could replace two men while eating only half as much.

Although the Army Air Forces got their quota increased by promising to pull onlyfrom its stations, the other branches struggled with the War Department over their requests.[12]

The same efficiency was seen in the other services. In 1944, the law was changed to allow Navy, Marine, and Coast Guard women to serve outside the continental United States. When SPAR telephone operators arrived in Hawaii, for the first time switchboards began to operate smoothly and people were actually able to get the parties they were calling.[13]

In February 1945, the 6888th Central Postal Battalion, an all-black female unit commanded by Maj. Charity Adams arrived in Europe to handle mail which had been misdirected under the original addresses. Pieces could potentially have gone to any American or Red Cross service member in the European Theater of Operations, approximately seven million people. A huge backlog of Christmas mail existed. The women worked seven days a week in three 8-hour shifts to clear it up, with each shift processing 65,000 pieces. The unit moved operations to Rouen and finally Paris. The efficiency of the unit remained high because the WACs understood the importance of letters and packages from home.[14]

In December 1944, a hospital commanding officer in Europe commented that the nurses were not only important in terms of the help they gave the doctors, but that "the nurse gives the soldier the L.T.C. he needs so badly and that is often the difference between life and death. What is L.T.C.? Oh, it's 'loving, tender care.'" Put a different way, "The presence of nurses at the front improved the morale of all fighting men because soldiers realized that they would receive skilled care in the event they were wounded. Hospitalized men recovered sooner when nurses cared for them. Troops in the field figured that "if the nurses can take it, then we can."[15]

Although in the minority, women also served in non-traditional roles in all the services. WACs and WAVES became mechanics, gunnery instructors, communications officers, intelligence analysts, photographers, printers, operating room technicians, carpenters, painters, parachute riggers, and heavy equipment operators. Women Marines became quartermasters, truck drivers, telegraph operators, motion picture operators, bakers, and agriculturists. SPARs became electricians, cooks, pharmacist mates, radio technicians, and machinist mates.[16]

The armed forces also inducted, albeit sometimes reluctantly, members of professions--doctors, lawyers, engineers, and at least one female ship captain. Because of the services' early refusal to take women doctors, talent was obviously wasted. Although a physician, Pvt. Lucille McClarren of Pennsylvania was working as a secretary in the War Department prior to joining the Marines on the first day of enlistment. In August 1943, she became the Corps' first woman sergeant. In April 1943, a special act was passed by Congress to allow the military to commission women doctors. Approximately one hundred served. In 1942, Elsa Gardner was the only woman aeronautical engineer serving in the Navy. She was a WAC sergeant with expertise in bridge demolition and was directly commissioned as a Major in the Corps of Engineers. In 1944 Capt. Lily Hutcheon of California, a lawyer, became the Marine Corps' first Judge Advocate. On May 24, she reported for duty as Acting Judge Advocate before the General Court Martial Board and Legal Assistance Officer at Camp LeJeune. D'Arcy Grant Parrott had been a licensed Chesapeake Bay schooner captain prior to joining the Coast Guard at Baltimore in 1943.[17]

Women Air Force Service Pilots, in cockpit of Curtis A25A
Navy dive bombers on orders by the Army. 50th Anniversary
of WWII Commemoration Committee.

Grumman Aircraft women test pilots: Barbara Jayne (left),
Elizabeth Hooker (center), Cecil "Teddy Kenyon (right.
Kenyon had also flown for the civil air patrol. Northrop
Grumman Corp., Bethpage, NY

10

Women in Aviation

From its early beginnings in the first decades of the twentieth century, the field of aviation involved women. In 1911, Harriet Quimby was the first female licensed pilot. By 1929, many more women had entered the field. That year, the first women's air race was held between Santa Monica, California and Cleveland, Ohio. In 1932, Amelia Earhart was the first woman to make a solo flight across the Atlantic. In 1936, Louise Thadden won the transcontinental Bendix Race, beating a field of men. There were women barnstormers and stunt fliers, among them Bessie Coleman, a black aviator, who was killed rehearing for a performance. By 1940, the Ninety-Nines, a women's pilot group founded by Amelia Earhart, had more than four hundred members.[1]

When World War II broke out, Gen. Henry (Hap) Arnold, chief of the Army Air Corps was open to the use of women in aviation specialties, including as pilots. Jacqueline Cochran and Nancy

Love, both experienced pilots, provided the leadership which established the Women Air Force Service Pilot (WASPs) program.

Jacqueline Cochran was then president of the Ninety-Nines, holder of several women's speed records and of the 1938 and 1939 Harmon Trophies, given by the International League of Aviators to the outstanding woman pilot of the year. She had been promoting the organization of a women's pilot group within the Air Corps, however Arnold did not think the moment ripe. Growing up in an impoverished home in Florida, starting at age eleven, Cochran trained as a beautician and worked seasonally in Miami and New York City. Invited to a social function one night by one of her clients, she met financier Floyd Odlum, president of the Atlas and Utilities Investment Corporation. Cochran told Odlum she intended to start her own cosmetics busines and he casually suggested that learning to fly would help. In 1932, Cochran received a pilot's license after taking three weeks of lessons at Roosevelt Field on Long Island. In 1936, Cochran and Odlum were married. He served as her entree to the highest social and political circles in the country.

Even before the war, Cochran foresaw the contribution that could be made by women pilots. She wrote Eleanor Roosevelt that the real bottleneck in wartime aviation would be trained pilots. In 1941, she completed a report for General Arnold proposing the organization of a woman pilot's division of the Air Corps Ferrying Command. In the meantime, as Britain had opened positions for women pilots in its Air Transport Auxiliary (ATA). Cochran recruited twenty-four women pilots who, after being checked out in Canada, flew to England and began to fly for the ATA in the spring of 1942. Their basic assignment was to ferry aircraft from factories to air bases around Britain. The women committed to eighteen months of service, and four stayed until 1945.

In September 1942, Cochran returned to the United States with the understanding that General Arnold had promised her the directorship of a woman's pilot group. When Cochran arrived, she found herself embroiled in a struggle over leadership.

In the spring of 1942, Col. William H. Tunner, head of the domestic wing of the Ferrying Division of the newly constituted Air Transport Command (ATC), had been introduced to Nancy

Love through her husband Robert, one of his colleagues. Mrs. Love had suggested the use of women pilots earlier, and now was invited to make a new proposal.

Nancy Harkness Love learned to fly at age sixteen in Houghton, Michigan and received her commercial license while in college. She was educated in private schools, although she was forced to drop out of Vassar after her sophomore year for financial reasons. In 1936 she married Robert Love. While on their honeymoon, the Beechcraft Corporation entered her in the National Air Races in Los Angeles. Because of her inexperience with pylon flying, she tried to back out without success and she finished fifth in the race. She and her husband started an aircraft sales company, which they were running when the war in Europe broke out.

By June 1940, Love was already in contact with the Air Corps Ferrying Command when she was one of a group of pilots who flew American airplanes to the Canadian border, landed them, and physically pushed them into Canada. They then flew them to Canadian bases where they awaited shipment to France. If U.S. pilots had flown war planes over the border that would have violated the country's neutral status.

When Robert Love was called to active duty, the couple moved to Washington, D.C. where Nancy began work as a civilian employee in the ATC. Through the encouragement of Colonel Tunner, in the summer of 1942 Gen. Harold George, head of the ATC, requested Nancy Love to make a proposal for the use of women pilots. Changes made by Tunner in the version submitted to George required that the women meet higher standards than the male pilots in terms of education and flight hours. September 5, 1942, General George, activated the Women's Auxiliary Ferrying Squadron (WAFS), under the direction of Nancy Love. It would be comprised of civilian pilots contracted by the Army Air Forces.

That same month Cochran returned to the United States and discovered that her anticipated position had been assigned to another woman. As an interim compromise, General Arnold made Cochran head of a training program known as the Women's Flying Training Detachment (WFTD). The first training school was set up in Houston, Texas, which was later moved to Avenger Field in Sweetwater, Texas. The first class graduated in April 1943.

Love's elite group of experienced, hand-picked pilots was the first off the ground on October 20, 1942. The ATC instructors had trained the women in military flying procedures and ran them through tests and classes. Within forty days from the time the first invitations to apply went out, the women were ferrying aircraft. Some of the women had more experience than their instructors. In the first few months, they achieved a 100 percent delivery rate. They also operated from an increased number of bases. In March 1944, Barbara Erickson was awarded the Air Medal by General Arnold, along with a Presidential citation, for ferrying three different aircraft in four 2,000- mile flights within a period of five days.

Also in October, the Cochran group came to Houston at their own expense for five months' training. They and subsequent graduates were assigned to duty with the WAFS. Then August of 1943, the WAFS were placed under a new organization, the Women Air Force Service Pilots (WASPs) under Jacqueline Cochran. Nancy Love, still in charge of the women from the ATC Ferrying Division, now reported to Cochran. Only the first twenty-seven WAFS retained their original unit name.

Within the first year, Cochran began to urge the expansion of the women's duties. The WASP's first new duty was target towing. A long strip of fabric was towed behind a plane for practice inantiaircraft gunnery. The women later flew planes for training in searchlight tracking and strafing. They flew radar missions and remote-control drone planes. Some WASPs flew weather planes and delivered cargo. They also tested new aircraft. Ann Carl became the first woman, and one of the few pilots, to test fly the Bell YP-59, the first jet fighter.

The women were allowed to increase the types of planes they could pilot. They started with trainers and liaison aircraft. By 1944, 123 were qualified in P-47 Thunderbolt fighters and others piloted B-17, B-26, and B-29 bombers. In the case of the B-26 and B-29, the women were trained specifically in testing to serve as examples to the men who found the planes difficult and dangerous to fly. Many WASPs were rated to fly on instruments only.

In 1944, General Arnold submitted legislation to the Congress to incorporate the WASP program into the Army Air Forces. The bill was voted down and the program was disbanded as of December 20, 1944. By that time 1,074 women had flown for the AAF, having logged over 60 million miles in almost every type of aircraft the Army owned. Eleven women were killed during training and another tenty-seven on duty. It was suspected that a few deaths were due to sabotage.

As civilian employees, the women received no death or veterans benefits, although these were conferred by special legislation in 1977. Some of the women continued to fly the rest of their lives. This author met one at an airshow in 1987. She was seventy-three at the time and had to go home early because she had been called out on a Civil Air Patrol search. Aside from their outstanding wartime record, these women also broke down the doors of the all-male military flying club. More would be admitted in the 1970s when the services opened flight schools to women.[2]

During the war, large numbers of other service women filled aviation positions. Approximately35 percent of the WACs served with the Army Air Forces (as compared with the Army Service Forces and the Army Ground Forces). About one half were assigned to clerical or administrative positions. The AAF placed more in technical specialties when a shortage of male recruits who scored high enough on aptitude tests to qualify later developed.

Air WACs worked as air traffic controllers, Link trainer instructors, aerial photographers, bombsight maintenance specialists, weather observers and forecasters, sheet metal workers, and radio operators. Some women flew training and administrative missions as crew members, radio operators, mechanics, and flight clerks. During the war, three were awarded the Air Medal. One winner received it for her work mapping the "Hump," the mountain supply route flown from Burma into China.[3]

The Navy was equally welcoming to women in aviation. Joy Bright Hancock, a World War I Navy veteran, pilot, and civilian employee in the Bureau of Aeronautics (BuAir), had helped plan the WAVES. As a new WAVES officer, she became representative to the BuAir chief, which put her in a position to influence the assignment of WAVES to aviation billets. More than one in four ended up with aviation positions.

WAVES officers served in aerological and aeronautical engineering, air combat information, aerial gunnery instruction, air transportation, celestial air navigation, Link training, plane recognition, flight scheduling and records, air transport radar, and air traffic control positions. Enlisted women, who were mostly high school graduates, served as aerographer mates, aviation machinist mates, aviation metalsmiths, parachute riggers, navigational aids instructors, electronic technician mates, aviation ordnancemen, and transport airmen.

WAVES served as flight crew members on noncombat aircraft. As of August 1945, eighty officers had become the first female military navigators on flights going to the Aleutians, Hawaii, and other destinations. Navigation instructors were required to put in fifty hours of flight time. Women parachute riggers also found themselves in the air. Although not at first required, ultimately the women had to make at least one jump with a chute they had personally packed. Air traffic controllers, who had to master regulations, procedures, and charts and learn meteorology, found their worst problem was climbing the towers in skirts. Pants were issued later.

Navy women working as aviation machinist's mates could find their jobs challenging, but in a different way. A visitor to one training site was quoted:

> In the engine shop, former school teachers, shop girls, and debutantes learn to tear down a giant airplane engine of about 3,000 parts and put it back together again. With engines roaring and props spinning, a harassed student may suddenly hear an offbeat, and it's up to her to find its ailment. Frequently, it is a wad of chewing gum purposely stuck over a fuel vent by an instructor.

The smaller Marine Corps and Coast Guard used women in similar roles in the aviation field. One third of the Women Marines filled aviation positions. At the largest Marine Corps Air Station at Cherry Point, North Carolina more than 2,500 women at the peak in 1944 made up 10 percent of assigned personnel. Women accounted for nine out of ten parachute riggers and eight out of ten control tower operators. They constituted all the Link trainer instructors and many were air gunnery instructors. Women Marines in salvage sections stripped damaged planes for usable parts and shipped them to Navy Supply to rebuild aircraft. Coast Guard SPARs and temporary reservists worked with regular, reserve and auxiliary units which conducted search and rescue missions for on-the-water plane crashes and salvaged submerged planes.[4]

Civilian women backed up military operations. CAP pilots flew search and rescue missions for downed military pilots. As of December 1942, a small group of women from the West and Midwest had become members of the San Diego parachute medical unit of the California Women's Ambulance and Transport Corps. They apparently were trained to parachute into the California mountains to give immediate medical treatment to crashed fliers. It is not clear whether these plucky efforts would have been successful or long-lasting. During the war, there were thousands of training flight crashes. If fliers crashed into mountains, most would probably have been killed. A high number of parachutists might have been injured during training. Such groups may not have been found cost effective. On the other hand, medics were dropped into mountain areas in the Pacific. The best guess is that such parachute groups would have been effective if, the jumpers had been previously trained, they could operate on call, and if there were no other way to get immediate medical treatment to an air crew.

Willa Brown was a CAP lieutenant and the director of and instructor at the Coffey School of Aeronautics in Oak Lawn, Illinois, the first owned and operated by African-Americans. Some of the graduates of her school became Tuskegee Fliers, the famous black pilots who served in Europe. Janet Harmon and a partner also set up a similar interracial aviation school at the same airport for those not eligible to enter the Coffey program. Evelyn Kilgore, Edna Gardner, and Arlene Davis trained military pilots.[5]

Coast Guard SPAR radio watchstander. Operators handled distress, security, and operations message traffic from ships at sea. U.S. Coast Guard, Historian's Office

11

Dawn of
the Electronic Age

Electronics was another field which achieved breakthroughs during the war. By 1941, in the United States, radio communications systems were in wide military use. Enemy detection was aided by the development of radar, which relied on pulse transmissions of radio signals to locate aircraft and submarines by visual means. Radio messages were encoded and encrypted. The need to decrypt large volumes of message traffic, particularly from enemy vessels, provided the impetus for the development of electronic signal processing--the basis of modern computers. This technology was also used in weapons development and testing. During the war, women were involved in the development, operation, and maintenance of all these systems.

Women were utilized heavily in communication positions. By 1945, 80 percent of the Navy Headquarters communications staff were WAVES. One hundred and twenty-one WAVES officers were trained to administer the Navy's radio-radar program. In 1944, 23 percent of SPAR officers were assigned to communications.

Women were heavily involved in code and code-breaking work. In the Navy Headquarters code rooms, they ran the machines that did all the encoding and decoding. By 1945, the Navy possessed the precursor of an electronic computer, which the women operated, that sorted and analyzed letter and cipher frequencies. Certain letters occur with predictable mathematical frequencies in differentl languages. By determining frequency clues are given to the text of secret transmissions.

Agnes Myer Driscoll had been working on cipher machines since the 1920s. As a civilian employee, she continued intelligence work with the Navy prior to the war, trying to read Japanese naval message traffic. By the beginning of 1942, "the immensely talented duo of [Driscoll] and Commander Joseph Rochefort had both succeeded . . . in making partial manual penetration of the naval ciphers."[1]

In New Guinea, a group of twenty WACs decoded Japanese radio traffic through their knowledge of the language. They worked on the "water codes" used by merchant ships en route from Japan with troops and supplies. Once enough information had been gleaned, it was transmitted to Navy submarines, which were quite successful in sinking the ships. The women's group became known to the Japanese, and "Tokyo Rose" broadcast that the unit would be attacked by Japanese aircraft. When Corp. Ginny Blakemore was told of the threat, she didn't know whether to trust American forces to defend her or to seek shelter for the night elsewhere. "Some of the girls went to spend the night in the ravine nearby, but there were tarantulas and boa constrictors down there! I decided not to, went to my tent, tucked in my mosquito netting, and went to sleep singing the hymn, 'Be Not Dismayed What Ere Betide, God Will Take Care of You.'" American planes turned back the Japanese aircraft, and the attack never materialized. The next morning, the women who had spent the night in the ravine emerged dirty and sleepless. When Blakemore saw them, she thought that there are no atheists either in ravines or foxholes.

The decoding work these women did was among the most important intelligence work of the war. With the sinking of merchant vessels, Japanese troops on islands could not be reinforced and the Japan mainland suffered for want of goods. After the war, General Tojo said that the decimation of the merchant marine was one of three major reasons for Japan's defeat. Japanese submarines never targeted American merchant ships to the same extent.[2]

One top secret development was a radio navigation system known as Loran (long range aid to navigation). By analyzing the difference in timing of signals from two separate shore stations, crews on ships and planes could determine their location in terms of longitude and latitude. The Coast Guard Loran monitor station at Chatham, Massachusetts was manned solely by women. Here they took readings of the radio signals being transmitted by the shore stations, every two minutes, twenty-four hours a day, to check for accuracy and operation. Commanding officer, Lt. (jg.) Vera Hamerschlagg remembered looking up at the 125-foot antenna mast and wondering:

> which SPAR would climb the riggin' if something went wrong. I asked the CO whom I was replacing who took care of it. His nonchalant answer was not to worry since nothing would happen to it short of a hurricane. Well, we had [one] . . . the following fall during which operations were suspended and all hands evacuated in case the mast should topple over onto the buildings!

She summed up the women's contribution by writing, "Inasmuch as Loran is considered one of the outstanding scientific developments of this war, it is a satisfaction to know that Spars were given the opportunity to participate in its operation."[3]

In the area of computer technology, Grace Hopper was to have a legendary career in the Navy and became one of the people most responsible for the information revolution of the 1970s and 1980s. Hopper was born Grace Brewster Murray on December 9, 1906 in

New York City. She graduated Phi Beta Kappa from Vassar College and received a Ph.D. in mathematics from Yale. She taught at Barnard and Vassar Colleges until 1943. Joining the Navy, she took officer training at the Midshipmen's School in Northampton, Massachusetts. She was commissioned a lieutenant (jg.) and assigned to the Bureau of Ordnance Computation Project at Harvard University. There she worked as a programmer on the Mark 1, the first information-processing digital computer. Her team worked around the clock, operating the Mark 1. It was programmed to perform mathematical computations used in the development and testing of naval guns, mines, rockets, and ultimately the atomic bomb.

Hopper was discharged from active duty in 1946, but remained a reservist and continued to work on computers for the Navy. In 1949, she left the Harvard program to work for the Eckert Mauchly Corporation, which developed one of the world's first electronic computers. In 1966, Hopper retired from the Naval Reserve, but within a year was called back to active duty to direct a program to standardize the Navy's computer systems. In 1969, the Data Processing Management Association named her the first data processing "Man" of the Year. Hopper finally left the Navy in 1986, a rear admiral, at age eighty. She then became a consultant for the Digital Equipment Corporation. In 1991, President George Bush awarded Hopper the National Medal of Technology, the only time the medal was ever presented to an individual woman.

As part of her lifetime work in computers, Hopper helped develop the first practical compiler, a set of programs which translates written instructions into coded electronic signals by which a computer executes commands. She helped to formulate the programming language COBOL, which uses written statements that resemble English language sentences. Previous program languages had required the use of heavily coded statements. Once programs could be written in near-English, the number of people who could write them vastly expanded. As a result COBOL became the language used for most business applications such as payroll and personnel. This development, along with advances in hardware, stimulated the explosive growth in the use of computers from the 1970s on.

Hopper is also credited with coming up with the term "bug" to describe an error in a computer program. As she told it in August of 1945, while working on the Mark 1, "Things were going badly, there was something wrong in one of the circuits of the long, glass-enclosed computer. . . . Finally someone located the trouble spot, and using ordinary tweezers, removed the problem, a two-inch moth. From then on, when anything went wrong with a computer, we said it had bugs in it."

Grace Hopper, known to her staff as "Amazing Grace," died in January 1992, at age eighty-five. She had said that she wanted to live until the year 2000 for two reasons: "The first is that the party on December 31, 1999 will be the New Year's Eve party to end all New Year's Eve parties. The second is that I want to point back to the early days of computers and say to all the doubters, 'See! We told you the computer could do all that.'"[4]

12

Women and Weaponry

Although women were allowed to fill only noncombat positions, this restriction did not preclude them from serving as gunnery instructors, repairing and handling ordnance, or carrying and using arms in security positions. In basic training, Women Marines observed field demonstrations in the use of mortars, bazookas, flame-throwers, and weapons. Corps commanders wanted to instill the traditional Marine *esprit de corps* and to have the women "see the faces of the young men they would free to fight."

WAVES and Women Marines served as aerial gunnery instructors at air stations around the country. Women Marines "fixed gunnery" trainers taught pilots how to shoot down planes. Most had had flight training or had taken ground school courses as civilians. The free gunnery instructors taught air crews who manned turret guns. They instructed in range and recognition, sights, aerial gunnery theory, deflection firing and turret control.

As for the WACs, the Army had to overcome public relations problems involving women and weapons. Finance, signal corps, and communications personnel had to have weapons available to guard payrolls, code rooms, and dispatches. In overseas areas, vehicles could not be taken out without arms. Some Air Forces instructors also needed weapon models. So women filling these positions received arms training, usually with a .45-caliber automatic pistol, the standard issue officer sidearm, and carried arms when required. In addition, the War Department took little notice of the few women marksmen who were putting in a little practice. Other WACs liked the training the men were willing to give them in their spare time. A backlash was created, however, when a few newspaper photographs of the women were printed. Disapproval hinged on ideas that they were being trained for combat, that they did not have anything better to do than engage in sport, and that they were wasting ammunition.

In response to the public outcry, Colonel Hobby obtained approval for a total ban on the women's use of weapons or anything that resembled them. After receiving complaints from commanding officers, however, Hobby made repeated requests to modify the policy. Finally, a circular was issued which gave commanding generals discretion to name specific persons who qualified in the use of arms. Six months later this was rescinded after it was found that, "WAC personnel are being required to drill in the use of arms and at some localities, there is wholesale participation by WAC personnel in familiarization courses in the use of weapons and arms." After this authorization was abolished, only a policy which stated that women who qualified for marksmen badges couldn't wear them was left standing. In practice, however, those women assigned to positions which required use of a weapon continued to receive training.[1]

The services under Naval command did not seem to have such problems. Soon after the Women's Reserve training school was established at Mount Holyoke, the Marine Corps commanding officer wrote his superior:

> In drawing these up [training schedules], I found myself wishing more and more that we could include some weapons

instructions, at least pistols, for our women. . . . I have found that the women come into the Marine Corps expecting to learn to shoot and I, of course, would like to see them become the first women's reserve in the country to take up the specialty of their men. . . . I wouldn't have had the nerve to suggest it if Mrs. Franklin D. Roosevelt hadn't asked me on her visit last week how soon they were goiong to learn to shoot. She expressed surprise at learning that the women of the U.S. were not learning as much about weapons, as the women of other countries.[2]

Navy, Marine, and Coast Guard communications officers who carried secret documents, and individual and group orders wore sidearms; SPARs served as armed guards. It is assumed that Navy regulations, like those of the Army, would have required that weapons be available to guard payrolls and code rooms. (No mention is made of a weapons policy in the WAVES administration history.)[3]

Another little known group of women who received small arms training consisted of Coast Guard Women temporary Reservists working in Volunteer Port Security Force (VPSF) units. These operated under their own command structure in twenty-two port cities. Men and women served on a part-time basis guarding ports and docks. Over a three year period, the Philadelphia group put in three million man hours. In New Orleans, ten married couples enrolled. Nationwide, overtwo thousand women joined. The units' main duties were to protect ships, docks, and cargo from fire and sabotage. During the war, thousands of tons of ammunition and bombs were loaded and unloaded and shipped from American ports. If one explosion on one ship had occurred, whole sections of a city could have been destroyed. VPSF volunteers also made arrests and assisted with drownings and other medical, fire, and storm emergencies.

In some of the VPSF units, the women received the same training as the men inareas such as the chemistry of fire, German sabotage methods, and handling dangerous cargo. Although the women mostly carried out administrative duties, they also served as drivers, messengers, and auto mechanics. They received small arms training and a number became proficient marksmen.[4]

In spite of their noncombatant status, the Army did conduct one experiment that employed WAACs in a combat-related role. In January 1943, ten officers and more than 200 enlisted women replaced men in two top secret antiaircraft batteries in the Washington, D.C. area. The women received on-the-job training in more than half the positions. They were not assigned to the 90-mm. gun or to outlying searchlight locations. In assessing the women's performance, the battalion commander reported that the women were very capable, especially in operating radar, determining the altitude and direction of incoming aircraft and controlling the searchlights. He recommended retaining the women and requested ten times as many. In spite of the success of the experiment, the chief of staff decided that the women would be most effectively employed if they remained in administrative and logistical positions. The threat of enemy attack on the mainland had subsided by that point in the war and the mobilization of troops for combat overseas had been given priority.[5]

Women Marines attach a depth bomb to the bomb rack of an airplane while attending Ordnance School at the Marine Corps Air Station in Quantico, Va. in August 1944. National Archives,

13

Over There

Once the women began to be assigned in large numbers overseas, the greatest dangers they faced were those from torpedoes, bombs, enemy aircraft, and disease. In the early morning hours of November 8, 1942, sixty nurses with the 48th Surgical Hospital landed with the first amphibious troops on the beaches of North Africa near Arzew, Algeria. Amidst sniper fire, the assault troops and medical crews who waded ashore sought cover behind sand dunes. Later, under cover of darkness they occupied beach houses, and then moved to an abandoned hospital.

Dr. Edward Rosenbaum recalled that when told six nurses were going with his medical unit which was to land near Oran, he thought he would not be in great danger. Upon disembarking, the first artillery shell splashed in the water near his ship and the next one was a direct hit, producing a gaping hole in the deck and killing a crewman. Rosenbaum found himself frantically climbing down the ship's rope ladders to the landing craft below. Next to him was Lt. Vilma Vogler of the Army Nurse Corps. They exchanged shocked glances and continued their descent. Said he, "At that moment she and the other nurses had ceased to be 'the women.' We were all comrades on equally dangerous footing, trying to survive the insanity of combat." By the time the medical team reached shore, the beach had been secured. They moved inland with the infantry and set up a hospital in a French Foreign Legion barracks.

For the first week, medical staff found themselves working twenty-four hours a day. The only medical supplies were those they had brought with them, so they immediately became short of bandages and sedatives. Nurses used their underclothes for bandages and gave their C rations to the wounded. At Arzew, bombings by enemy aircraft held up delivery of supplies for two days. They quickly ran out of beds, and men lay in pools of blood on the floor. There was no electricity or running water and doctors operated with the only light supplied by flashlights.[1]

As the nurses were coping with the casualties and primitive conditions, the first WAAC officers arrived overseas in December. Only the most highly qualified received these assignments. Five captains, two of whom were bilingual, were qualified to act as executive secretaries. They made an unexpected entrance into the theater after their ship was sunk by a enemy action. Two were rescued from the burning deck. The other three made it into lifeboats and rescued several sailors by pulling them in with them. A destroyer picked them up and delivered them to Algiers with no clothing or supplies where Army officers gave them gifts of oranges and toiletries.

In January 1943, 196 WAACs of the 149th WAAC Post Headquarters Company arrived to serve in General Eisenhower's theater headquarters in Algiers. These 196 women served as clerks, stenographers, switchboard operators, typists, and drivers. When Colonel Hobby had requested volunteers from the 1st WAAC Separate Battalion in Florida, all had responded. In the spring, WAACs arrived monthly to staff the 5th Army Headquarters in Morocco and the 12th Air Force Headquarters in Algeria. WAAC Ethel Horton wrote that when she would make long distance telephone calls, the officer would answer, drop the phone, and gasp, "A woman's voice! She speaks ENGLISH!"[2]

In January, the Allies were also engaged in the Tunisian campaign. This called for an eastward advance by land across northern Algeria. Amphibious landings were considered too risky, as the Germans could receive air support from Sicily. The nurses moved with the troops, sleeping on the ground or in tents. The initial objectives were the northern port cities of Bizerte and Tunis. Near the end of January, the chief focus changed to central Tunisia to prevent a linkup between the forces of General Field Marshall Erwin Rommel'and General von Arnim moving westward from Libya.

By February, the fighting centered around the town of Faid. There, the Axis were able to counter the Allied advance. In a series of attacks from February 14 to 16, they pushed the Allied line back approximately thirty-five miles to Sbeitla. The Americans fell back to establish a new defensive line at the Kasserine Pass. During the Allied withdrawal, German flank advances were so rapid that for a while medical units were trapped in front of Allied lines. The nurses volunteered to stay with the wounded and ultimately were the "last ones to come back" within American lines.[3]

The North African campaign tested the Army Medical Department's newly organized "chain of evacuation" hospital system. This was a cascading system of mobile and base hospitals through which patients passed from the front lines back to recuperation hospitals in occupied areas. The field hospitals, which operated anywhere from two to twenty miles behind the front lines were made up of tents holding 75 to 150 patients. Eighteen nurses were usually assigned. Here the wounded came by ambulances and litter and triage was performed. This was an initial assessment of the severity of a patient's condition and the type of treatment required. Depending on the evaluation, patients either went directly into surgery or were stabilized and sent to evacuation hospitals farther away from the front. At the evacuation hospital which could manage 750 patients and had fifty-three nurses, operations were performed and patients were sent to the rear by air or ship depending on their condition. Station hospitals and general hospitals were housed in semipermanent locations, usually in converted buildings with electricity and running water. Even these were frequently subject to enemy air attacks. Patients from these hospitals might besent backto duty or home to the United States.

All hospitals were subject to enemy bombing. Those on the front lines were strafed and threatened with encirclement by enemy troops. The 48th Surgical Hospital at Gafsa, Tunisia was located in a heavily targeted area between an airfield and an ammunition dump. Facilities could be moved as many as two times in one week. The 77th Evacuation Hospital near Tebessa, informed of a German breakthrough at the Kasserine Pass packed up and moved 150 patients sixty miles to a safer area. The new unit was fully operational again within twelve hours.[4]

Patients could be evacuated by air, ship, or train, and nurses served on all of these modes of transportation. On trains, staff made patients comfortable, gave food and medicine, and watched for signs of changed conditions, stress, or complications. Hospital ships were painted white with large red crosses on either side and were supposed to be off limits to enemy attack. The planes were not marked since they doubled as cargo planes. When they flew with patients, they were subject to enemy fire.

Flight nurses were specially trained for their work. They had to be in peak physical condition; training focused on crash procedures, survival in the ocean, jungle, desert, and arctic environments, and the effects of altitude on patients. The nurses went through parachute drills, simulated bombings, and strafings.

Prior to flight, the nurses were briefed by doctors on the condition of each patient. Flying could cause unique care problems. Air sickness in a patient with a wired jaw could cause him to breathe in vomit and asphyxiate. Combat stress in soldiers meant they had to be strapped into their litters. Changes in high altitudes required knowledge of the correct dosages of medicine, which could be different at different heights. Lack of equipment coulc be a problem. One nurse had to hack away at a cast with bandage scissors when the patient began to hemorrhage beneath it. She eventually removed the cast and stopped the bleeding. The C-46, one of the evacuation planes, was known as the "flying coffin" since its heater sometimes caused the plane to explode in midair. Ssome pilots refused to turn on their heaters during flight, making it difficult for the nurses to keep warm critically ill patients.

During the war, the five hundred flight nurses who served in the thirty-one transport squadrons achieved a remarkable evacuation record. Worldwide, only forty-six out of 1,176,048 patients died in flight. Seventeen of the flight nurses were killed.

Air evacuations began in North Africa in February 1943, and eventually became part of every theater of operations. In August 1943, second Lt. Sylvia Van Antwerp filed a report from Tunisia with the *New York Times*. In less than two months 18,000 men had been evacuated in DC-3 aircraft. Each DC-3 carried seventeen men.

Antwerp had been a flight attendant for a commercial airline before the war who stated that her civilian passengers had given her more problems than the wounded. Badly wounded soldiers were very patient and would often tell her that they didn't "want to cause trouble." Sometimes she had to stay overnight at an advanced airfield. The men tried to give her good accommodations, but as she said, she didn't care where she slept. "It was beautiful there, with the mountains all around. In the night, you could hear the guns rumbling in the mountains past Beja. At dawn long strings of ambulances come down the roads toward the airfield." To date, she had only been strafed once, on the ground. "I lay in a slit trench and listened to the bullets rip into the hard baked dirt of the flying field." Other nurses she knew had been attacked in the air.[5]

Later in the war, Navy nurses arrived in North Africa. Beginning in the spring of 1944, twenty-five staffed the base hospital in Oran, Algeria. Navy nurses were also assigned in Bizerte, Palermo and Naples.[6]

Also in North Africa was Josephine Baker, the legendary American-born Parisian cabaret singer and dancer who had become a French citizen in 1937. In 1939, agent Jacques Abtey asked Baker to enlist in the Free French secret service to gather information as she conducted her show tours. Her patriotic response was, "France made me what I am. . . .The Parisians gave me their hearts, and I am ready to give them my life." In October 1940, Baker and Abtey left France for Lisbon, with Abtey posing as her ballet master and carrying secret service documents. For the remainder of the war, Baker divided her time between Lisbon and North Africa. She gathered intelligence, obtained passports for escaping Jews, arranged discreet diplomatic meetings, and entertained American throughout the Middle East. While traveling, Baker wore an army overcoat and helmet and knitted. One colleague described their venture, "The blazing heat of day, the cold nights, sand fleas...the desert strewn with the twisted remains of tanks. . . .In that cruel landscape we took turns keeping watch at night to ward off scavengers who preyed on corpses and would have preyed on us as well." Having become a symbol of Free France, and probably normality, Baker made a triumphant return to a liberated Paris in October 1944. One million people lined the Champs-Elysees to see her enter the city and she was barraged with flowers. In 1961, the French government awarded Baker the Legion of Honor and the Croix de Guerre with palm for her war-time services.[7]

Hospital dietician, physical therapist, and army nurses model new uniforms at the Franco-American-British Medical Corps Clinical Conference held in Oran, North Africa, November 1943

14

The European Mainland

During the summer of 1943, the first WACs began arriving in England. Their assignments included Supreme Headquarters, Allied Expeditionary Force; European Theater of Operations; Strategic Air Forces; the 8th Fighter and 9th Bomber Commands; the American Expeditionary Air Force; and the 8th and 9th Air Forces. They showed their courage under bombing and their efficiency as teleprinters, typists, switchboard operators, and photo interpreters. German bombing was sporadic, so the women became familiar with air raid shelters. Halfway around the world, WACs also arrived at the Southeast Asian Headquarters in India.[1]

On July 9, 1943, an Allied invasion force of 2,590 vessels sailed from North Africa to invade Sicily in one of the largest combined operations of World War II. Sicily would serve as a base for the invasion of Italy and a forefunner of the invasion of

Normandy in France the following year.[2] Nurses with the 10th Field and the 11th Evacuation Hospitals arrived three days later. The nurses spent time in slit trenches and foxholes, under fire from German Stuka dive bombers. Other nurses supporting the U.S. 7th Army were held up nine days awaiting transport, which was in short supply. While in Sicily, everyone suffered from the intense heat and a malaria epidemic broke out which soon spread to the medical staff. In spite of these conditions, the nurses at the 128th Evacuation Hospital worked 12-hour shifts, admitting three hundred patients a day.

Once Sicily was secure, American troops crossed to the Italian mainland at Salerno on September 8, 1943. General Eisenhower decided to wait until September 13 to land the nurses after a secure beachhead had been established. While making the crossing the night of September 13, the British hospital ship H.M.S *Newfoundland* was bombed, in spite of being marked with red crosses, and well lit. Before it sank, the 103 nurses on board were rescued and evacuated to Bizerte in Tunisia. Four had received minor wounds and were later awarded Purple Hearts. [3]

A first lieutenant from Iowa, whose ship was bombed en route to Bizerte, began work in a surprising state: "Wet and bedraggled, wearing nothing but pajamas with tennis shoes, she got ashore and was again at work." Another nurse from Maine concealed the back injury she had previously received. She jumped off her ship wearing her 55-pound pack. She worked until one leg became paralyzed. When the nurses arrived in Salerno, they were deluged with wounded and saw 12-to-20-hour days.[4]

A 60-WAC platoon of the 6669th Headquarters Company accompanied the 5th Army under Lt. Gen. Mark Clark as it crossed Algeria and went up the Italian peninsula. The thirty members who were assigned to advanced headquarters found themselves anywhere from six to thirteen miles behind the combat troops. They wore men's clothing and lived in whatever was available. During the 1944-45 winter, they lived in tents in the mountains above Florence. The women filled critical general support staff positions. They were said to be "perhaps the best integrated unit in the theater." Telephone operators were highly skilled, able to reach any field commander within minutes through a complicated communications network. Clerk-typists plotted the locations and movements of troops and supplies. The platoon was one of the few to receive both the 5th Army Plaque with clasp and the Meritorious Service Unit Plaque.[5]

Severe weather on the night of November 8, 1943, caused a famous episode in Army Nurse Corps history. A C-54 carrying thirteen flight nurses and thirteen medical corpsmen of the 807th Medical Air Evacuation Transport Squadron from Sicily to Bari on the Italian weast coast was forced down in the Albanian mountains in German occupied territory. Local guerrillas found the plane and took the Americans to a farmhouse. That night, the flight crew burned the aircraft to conceal their presence.

The nurses, corpsmen, and air crew then set out on what was to become an 800- mile journey of two months through winter weather and blinding snowstorms to Italy. Escorted by partisans, the members of the group suffered frostbite, dysentery, jaundice, and pneumonia. The main group of nurses arrived safely on January 9, 1944. Three who had been separated hid out in the home of a partisan in Albania for several months in the town of Berat. The resistance supplied them with civilian clothes and Albanian identification cards and they left in March by car. Reaching the interior, they rode donkeys across the mountain ranges and finally reached the coast. There, an Allied torpedo boat picked them up and took them to Otranto, Italy.[6]

To help overcome still German resistance on the west coast of Italy, the Allies executed a surprise invasion of the Anzio beachhead on January 22, 1944. Although the landing was initially successful, the Allies were pinned down in a small perimeter for four months, all the while repulsing persistent German air and ground attacks.

Three hospital units with approximately two hundred nurses landed with the first assault force. On the night of January 24, the Luftwaffe bombed three British hospital ships evacuating casualties from the beachhead. One, the H.M.S *St. David,* sank with 226 medical staff and patients on board. The two American nurses on board were among 130 survivors rescued. Second Lt. Ruth Hindman had also survived the sinking of the *Newfoundland.*

Other bombings took a greater toll. A direct hit on the surgical section of theU.S. 95th Evacuation Hospital killed three nurses and twenty-three other staff and patients; sixty-four others were wounded. Enemy artillery fire on February 10 hit the 33d Field Hospital. Two nurses and one enlisted man were killed, four medical officers and seven enlisted personnel were wounded. One of the shells hit the hospital tent generator starting a fire. Nurses helped evacuate forty-two patients safely. Four nurses--First Lt. Mary Roberts, Second Lt. Elvira Roe, Second Lt. Virginia Rourke and Second Lt. Ellen Ainsworth--received the Silver Star for their bravery in this incident (Ainsworth posthumously), the first of these awards ever given to women in the U.S. Army. The hospitals on the beachhead received direct hits through February and March. On March 29, the 56th Evacuation Hospital was shelled and three officers, one nurse, 14 enlisted men. and 19 patients were wounded. Four patients were killed.

Often the nurses and patients were unable even to take shelter during air raids. The hospital tents were eventually protected by foundations and earthworks, which protected them from shrapnel but not from bombs. Earlier, when shelling occurred, the nurses had to move immobile patients to the ground. Others hid under their beds. When patients couldn't be moved, the nurses stayed with them, using only their helmets for protection.

At Anzio, the Allied encampment was only fifteen miles wide by seven miles deep with the sea to the rear. There was no line of retreat. All airfield, batteries, ammunition dumps, and medical facilities were located close together. The medical facilities were frequently hit, earning their area the nickname, "Hell's Half Acre." Many soldiers believed they were safer in their foxholes than in the hospital. The nurses remained at Anzio because they were needed. Between January and June 1943, base hospitals admitted and evacuated more than 48,000 wounded, sick, and injured.[7]

While serving in Italy, First Lt. Cordelia Cook became the first nurse to receive a Bronze Star. She was also the first to receive two combat decorations, having previously been awarded a Purple Heart after her field hospital was bombed. The Bronze Star was awarded for her services in "direct support of combat operations" from November 1943 to January 1944, "during which time she was wounded by artillery fire and continued her duties."[8]

During the war, the Army honored its nurses by naming several hospital ships after them. On May 29, 1944, a converted Liberty ship was commissioned as a hospital ship, *The Blanche F. Sigman* in honor of First Lt. Sigman and her colleagues, First Lt. Carrie Sheetz, and Second Lt. Marjorie Morrow who were killed serving with the 95th Evacuation Hospital at Anzio. Near the end of 1944, one WAC officer and three enlisted women were assigned to the *Sigman* as radio operators. Later, secretaries and clerks came on board. WACs were also assigned in similar capacities on the hospital ships, *Larkspur* and *Charles E. Stafford.*[9]

Esther Richards, Red Cross worker who died at Anzio. American Red Cross.

Above: As the plane lands at Tacloban, Leyte, Philippine Islands, the first WAC detachment of the GHQ to arrive line up on the field. November 1944.

Below: WACs aboard the *Mactan* off the coast of Tacloban, Leyte, Philippine Islands, 1 January 1945.

15

Pacific and Far East

By mid-1944, WACs were being assigned to the Southwest Pacific Area (SWPA) under the command of Gen. Douglas MacArthur. In May 1944, they arrived in Australia and New Guinea. When MacArthur moved to retake the Philippines in October 1944,followed. The first WAC unit arrived in Manila three days after the Japanese evacuated. Eventually, 5,500 WACs were to serve in this theater, seventy percent in administrative and office positions. Some of the women were drivers and mechanics, retrained as office workers because as other theaters had stripped the cream and bulk of the crop of clerks and typists.

WACs serving in SWPA faced the greatest hardships in a daunting physical environment. The women's ingenuity, however, rose to meet theconditions. One unit, having been forewarned of the "wild country," disembarked in New Guinea with Australian laying hens and chicks (the hens laid no eggs thereafter). Others found no furniture in their quarters except cots, so they scavenged.

"The Quartermaster salvage dump proved a fascinating place," stated one WAC. Often dates would be chosen according to the furniture, construction materials, and/or labor skills to which potential suitors had access or possessed. WAC housing could eventually be found with dressing tables, wood floors, landscaping, and other appointments.[1]

Health problems were caused by the hot and humid climate, tropical diseases, lack of proper clothing, and poor food. The first items some women discarded were the winter uniforms, which they had been issued, complete with ski pants and ear muffs. All women in New Guinea were required to wear trousers for malarial control. Their heavy twill coveralls had not been designed for the tropics and skin diseases developed. The women switched to mens' khaki trousers which came to be in short supply. There was also a dearth of dry, high footgear which could be worn in foot-deep monsoon mud. Most women in the field subsisted on canned and dehydrated food or field rations, and many lost weight. The women had higher malaria rates than the men. This was mostly due to lack of light weight clothing and the failure of the women to properly wear the clothing against mosquitos. The women also suffered from pneumonia and bronchitis, as the humidity kept clothing wet.[2]

Long working hours and absence of leave time helped to push up the medical loss rate. The working day began at 7 or 8 a.m. and ended at 9 or 10 p.m. with three hours off for lunch during the midday heat, six days a week. When work was heavy, some women did not take lunch breaks. Two all-WAC units worked seven days a week for five months. A survey noted that, "In general, the enlisted women were working longer hours than enlisted men performing similar skilled duties."

Living conditions were also restrictive. Commanding officers in NewGuinea feared that the women--both WACS and nurses--would be assaulted by male soldiers, some of whom had not seen an American woman for over eighteen months. Therefore, the women were required to live in compounds enclosed in barbed wire and to be escorted to work and recreation facilities by armed guards. Both the women and their guards resented the system.

This system could be particularly demoralizing when coupled with confinement to the area and lack of outside recreation spots.

According to an Army historian, "During the entire stay in New Guinea, no leaves or passes were reported as given to enlisted women at most installations, because of the absence of approved places to spend them."[3]

Meanwhile, some four hundred WACs arrived in the China-Burma-India (CBI) theater in July 1944. They had been requisitioned to serve in the Army Air Forces headquarters in Calcutta. One-half were stenographers or typists, and the rest were highly skilled in other fields. Conditions here were less primitive, and the women were cordially welcomed. Toward the end of the war, about 100 WACs served in Chungking, China with AAF headquarters, and many stayed on when the headquarters moved to Shanghai with the defeat of Japan.

Army nurses served throughout SWPA and in the CBI theater. They endured every kind of hardship. In India, the nurses lived in "bashas," houses made of woven reeds with concrete floors. One nurse described her experience with scrub typhus which was spread by mites. "We averaged a casualty a day . . . So sick--very high fever, very often irrational. But it was a good nursing experience. You really felt like you were doing something when you were taking care of those fellows." She said few entertainment shows arrived in the CBI. "We were really at the end of the earth." Other diseases, such as dengue fever, malaria, and psychoses, were equally daunting, not to mention critical care of the wounded.[4]

Having survived the Pearl Harbor attack, the U.S.S. *Solace* was plying the waters of the Pacific. Until August 1942, the Navy Nurses on this ship were the only female naval personnel serving in the South Pacific. By the end of the war, Navy Nurses had been assigned to eleven hospital ships and to Pacific base hospitals in New Zealand, Australia, the Philippines and the islands of Efate, Espiritu Santo, Guadalcanal, Tulagi, New Guinea, Guam, Tinian, Saipan, and Manus.

As they had in Arica, flight nurses also operated in the Pacific theater. The first nurse to be killed in a theater of operations in the war was Second Lt. Ruth M. Gardiner. Her evacuation plane crashed near Nannek, Alaska on July 25, 1943. Then in December, Lt. Ernestine Koranda, was killed in a crash in the Pacific and a hospital ship was dedicated to her memory.[5]

By 1944, a modification to the ban on women serving on merchant vessels had been made. As a result, seven civilian nurses were assigned on ships operating from Alaskan ports. Maxine Lerch helped evacuate civilians and treated merchant mariners, servicemen and Japanese prisoners taken on the Aleutian Islands. When American troops occupied the island of Kiska, she was the first woman ashore. For her wartime activities, Lerch was awarded the U.S. Merchant Marine Emblem and the Pacific War Zone Bar for active service.

WAVES, SPARs and Women Marines were also assigned to Alaska and Hawaii. SPARs serving in Alaska in pay, personnel and communications ratings wore fur-lined parkas and heavy wool pants. In their spare time, they hiked in the mountains and visited nearby islands on Coast Guard cutters. The USO sponsored dances and the movie theater in Ketchikan had "cowboys on the screen and Indians in the seats."[6]

Army field medicine in its truest sense. Somewhere in the Southwest Pacific. U.S. Army, Center of Military History

16

The D Day Invasion

Gen. Dwight D. Eisenhower arrived in England in January 1944 to become Commander of SHAEF (Supreme Headquarters,Allied Expeditionary Force). His staff of British and American officers, assisted by military men and women with a range of special capabilities, setout to develop plans for the invasion of Normandy followed by a relentless advance into Germany.[1]

One of the key elements in planning the invasion was reliable intelligence, much of which came from the French Resistance. WAC stenographer Ruth Blanton was assigned to SHAEF Intelligence. She recorded, translated, and typed reports from the underground received by way of shortwave radio. Information included the number and location of sabotaged bridges and railroads; disposition and number of German troops; and activities and profiles of German officers. Each morning, intelligence officers presented to the general staff the reports Blanton had typed.

Each afternoon, Blanton updated the situation map which displayed battle lines and units engaged.[2]

WAC Major Mary Weems of Tennessee wrote home from London in April 1944, "Every General is screaming his head off for more WACS in his command and we just don't have them. What's wrong with the women in America? When I see these fliers over here with twelve and eighteen missions behind them and more to go, knowing that each one may be their last, I realize how little our government asks of women, and they aren't even willing to do that much. It just makes me ill."[3]

Although the WACs worked "around the clock throughout the planning period for D Day," they seemed to understand that if you had to be in a war, London was not a bad place to be. One wrote that part of the fun was that on any day, one could find oneself walking down a hallway and bumping into Jimmy Stewart or Clark Gable. Many movie stars joined the service as regular members or entertainers.[4]

The invasion was launched on June 6, 1944. The nurses were the first women to wade ashore on the Normandy beaches on D Day plus 4, June 10. They were part of the medical staff of the 42d and 45th Field Hospitals and the 91st and 128th Evacuation Hospitals. After coming ashore during the day, they slept on the beach that night. Others followed, and those who crossed the English Channel on the night of the 14thexperienced an attack on their convoy by German aircraft.[5]

Lt. Mary Louise Carpenter, ANC, left her English base on a warm day in a truck with the canvas sides rolled up. Her group was much cheered by the soldiers. Their ship arrived twenty-four hours later, and she found herself walking with her pack up a narrow road in Normandy, not quite knowing if it was the right road or where or how far the group was going. They finally arrived at a gathering of troops and equipment in a field, and the commanding officer came up and greeted them. In a letter written on July 31, she gave a clue as to how the nurses emotionally survived the continual ordeal of seeing dead and maimed young men: "It seems so remarkable when men who were moribund five days ago are eating and smiling that the nurses get almost slap happy at the relief and joy of it."[6]

Capt. Jean Truckey, ANC, of Detroit wrote a stream-of-consciousness letter home to her family on June 2:. "Shell pocked road signs reading, 'Roads Cleared of Mines to the Hedge.' Villages completely destroyed. Newly made graves. German and American helmets and equipment strewn everywhere. Colored parachutes dangling from trees. . . . Old orchards full of foxholes. Dead cattle and horses. Red and yellow roses climbing ancient stone walls."[7]

The first WAC unit arrived in France on D Day plus 38. Cpt. Isabel Kane wrote home on July 21 about the "open-mouthed amazement and howls of delight which came from the GIs along the roadside, as they recognized us. The grim, dogged looks changed as by a miracle into boyish grins and we were hailed all along the way, with shouts and welcome." She also stated she preferred living in the open in tents to the tension of London. She loved her field clothing and thanked her father for bringing her "up in the outdoors, for nothing here can phase me and I can take it all in stride."[8]

The women were not always cheery, especially those who were being bombed and strafed. Lt. June Wandrey, ANC, of Wisconsin wrote a discouraging letter home on August 3, 1944:

> Brother writes that I should rough it like he had to do recently, living in a tent--using a slit trench latrine, bathing out of a helmet, doing his own laundry. What does he think I've been doing in the past 19 months? Living in the open lots of times, pup tents, wall tents, finally a pyramidal, using slit trenches--lots of times without even a screen around it--bathing in a helmet, that is, if we could even spare the water, doing my own laundry, working 18-20 hours a day--living on "C" rations, seeing mangled young men about you at every turn. Trying to smile when all you wanted to do was to wash your face and curl up on the ground to get a bit of sleep--while the ground shook from artillery and the guards kept shouting--Air Raid--d---get those lights out and the flak fell all around and you hunched in a muddy foxhole wishing your steel helmet covered you from head to foot. Or you didn't have a

foxhole--you had to stay on the ward with the patients. They couldn't be moved and all any of you had for protection was that "beautiful" steel helmet, and you kept hearing the Jerries come over in a dive, and then the thrump of the bomb as it hit not far away--all the while our guns were putting a steady barrage of anti-aircraft fire. You just sat there hoping that their aim would be poor. I've lived that so long it has become part of me. When it's quiet, I worry--wonder what is going to happen.

Or some night to be getting a brief break from the O.R.--you step outside into the blackness only to see Jerry do strafing up and down the road a couple of hundred yards away from you. The bullets are beautiful streaks of red light as they come spitting death out of the plane earthward. So you cringe next to a tree hoping that he'll leave soon--or run out of ammunition. When it's over you get up and go back to the O Room. Already the casualties are coming in from the strafing--two are dead--one a chaplain--he was bending over and comforting a wounded lad when Jerry went over the Red Cross-marked clearing station next to your tentage. Oh, well . . .⁹

Carpenter seemed to take the bombing with a little more aplomb, at least on August 10. She wrote:

At six the next morning all of us became electrified into wide-awakeness as a whistle and a boom, and another and another told us German shells were coming into us and landing not far away. I rolled in my blankets from my cot on to the ground before the first landed, as they say the flatter one is in a shelling the better. . . . When the machine gun bullets seem to be flaying the air right over me and I hear a few of them whistle, I concentrate on hoping hard that fragments won't happen to strike the space of earth occupied by me, and, if I'm not on duty and a foxhole's handy, I get in.

Carpenter also wrote that "part of the great fun in coming here" was being treated like a conquering hero by the French people.[10]

These accounts show how close to the front lines nurses could be. Sometimes hospital staff would arrive so soon after fighting that they had to help bury the dead, or they would find the hospital ringed with artillery.[11]

Paris was liberated on August 25, 1944 and WAC units arrived less than a week after the Germans surrendered. By October, three thousand WACs were in France. [12] Some of the nurses received leaves and became tourists. Lt. Sally Zumaris was in Paris in December, but returned to her hospital when the Battle of the Bulge began. She reported, "After accidentally running into a gasoline dump near the front and a few other mishaps of black-out driving, we finally arrived in Ettelbruck, only to see artillery shooting in the direction of the hospital." When she reached her unit, she found only two officers and a few patients and she was sent to the rear, "and what a ride it was--all along the front lines--Jerry planes were overhead, anti-aircraft firing, M. P.s stopping us, asking for the password, and how surprised they'd be when they'd hear my faltering feminine voice."[13]

Meanwhile, flight nurses had been evacuating troops since D Day. Lt. Reba Z. Whittle crashed over Aachen in a C-47 behind enemy lines in September 1944. She and all other crew members were wounded. The Germans gave them medical treatment and imprisoned them in Stalag IXC. Whittle nursed the other captives throughout her five months' internment. She was released in January 1945.[14]

Lt. Aleda Lutz received the Distinguished Flying Cross posthumously. She was killed when her plane crashed in southern France in November 1944. By that time, she had completed 190 evacuation missions and had received the Air Medal with four Oak Leaf Clusters (one cluster signifies an additional award of the Air Medal). A former troopship was converted to a hospital ship and named after Lutz in February 1945.[15]

Back in London, the WACs were having a tough time of it, too. Within one week after the D Day invasion, the Germans launched their V-1 rocket attacks against Britain. This small, pilotless airplane detonated on contact and became known as the "buzz bomb." The V-2 rocket was launched in August. During flight it could not be heard but penetrated deeply into its target as it exploded, severely damaging buildings. The Americans and British had been bombling the sites of these weapons, which helped to delay their onslaught.[16]

Hitler hoped the bombs, essentially weapons of terror, would break the British morale. Commander Harry C. Butcher, General Eisenhower's naval aide, wrote in his diary, "most of the people I know are semi-dazed from loss of sleep and have the jitters, which they show when a door bangs or the sound of motors from motorcycles or aircraft are heard." He had counted twenty-five bombs which exploded within six hours in one night.[17]

On July 3, a V-1 fell on the quarters of American soldiers and WACs in London. The women administered first aid to the wounded and drove them to hospitals. They also set up a mess for civilian relief workers in their building. Of the 10,500 rockets launched, approximately20 percent scored hits, killing ten thousand people and destroying 1.1 million homes. Most of the Purple Hearts awarded to WACs were for wounds received during V-1 bombings in London.[18]

One WAC wrote home about the way she was coping with the tension:

At first they scared the living daylights out of us. I'll never forget the first night of them as long as I live. I don't know how many nights I slept in coveralls, field shoes, overcoat, helmet, and gas mask. In fact, I could hardly get into bed in such array. Lately, however, we have become more or less used to the buzz bombs and I have discarded all but the pajamas. Now when we hear them coming, everyone stays right in bed which after all, is as good a place as any. Everyone but me, that is. I have to get up and look for them.[19]

Navy Nurse Jean Kurtz worked at a base hospital in southern England. At first her group took precautions against the bombs too, and went to air raid shelters, but "the attacks were so frequent that finally we just remained on duty."[20]

At the Battle of the Bulge which began in mid-December 1944, the Germans launched their last desperate counteroffensive through a weak point in the Allied line in the Ardennes forest. Front line medical facilities were flooded with wounded. Lt. Evelyn Orth of Niagara Falls, New York wrote home toa friend from Germany in March 1945, describing her winter:

> I don't mind the tents much here because the weather has been nice but I sure hated it in Belgium all winter in tents with the old outfit . . . Many mornings we'd wake up and see 6 or 8 inches snow inside the tents . . .Then the buzz bombs came over day and night and then the German push and we didn't know half the time whether we were in front or behind the firing lines. We had to be ready to evacuate at a moments notice but we didn't have to and the only damage we got was a few torn tents and no casualties. My bed was busted up like kindling wood but I had crawled up out [of] bed 10 minutes before and was running like Hell when it hit. We were more fortunate than a lot however. [21]

Flying buzz bombs were not the only surprise Germans had for American nurses. On Easter Sunday 1945, a hospital convoy on the road near Nanau, Germany was ambushed by German troops. The ten nurses and other staff dove into a ditch to avoid the machine gun fire and then surrendered. The Germans took them to a nursing home and at gunpoint forced them to treat wounded. Nine hours later, the 5th Infantry freed the prisoners. On a lighter note, on March 28, 1945, Lt. Paula Krull of Massachusetts was traveling down a road in a jeep. Suddenly, two German soldiers burst out of the woods holding their rifles over their heads. In stumbling English, they announced, "We want to surrender to you because you are a lady and won't kill us." Krull ordered them to get on the hood of the jeep and directed her driver to take them to the 99th Division prison cage.[22]

When V-E Day was declared on May 8, 1945, there were 7,600 WACs and 17,000 Army nurses stationed in Europe along with Red Cross, OSS, and USO personnel. Many WACs had turned down offers of promotion and admittance to Officers' Candidate School to accept jobs overseas. The women had shown themselves to be excellent ambassadors.[23]

Army nurses sandbagging tents.   Location/date unknown.   U.S. Army, Center of Military History

17

American Women in the French Resistance

From the time Hitler invaded France, Belgium, the Netherlands, Luxembourg, Denmark and Norway, the citizens of these countries had been working with British and American intelligence, supplying information on German movements, sabotaging military operations, and helping downed air crews return to Britain. By 1944, France had 177 networks and subgroups, forty-one resistance movements, hundreds of underground newspapers and 200,000 guerrillas, all of whom helped five thousand airmen escape. Prior to D Day, these groups had been working for months, planning their activities to coordinate with Allied troop movements. Although these nationalist movements are well known today through the media, the part played by American women is not so well known.

American women supplied intelligence, worked as couriers and safehouse keepers, engaged in sabotage and guerrilla activities, and aided air crews. The most notable was Virginia Hall. She was born in Baltimore in 1906 to a prominent family, attended school in Europe, and was fluent in French, German, and Italian. After having failed to gain a Foreign Service appointment after passing the exam, she obtained a clerical position in the U.S. State Department.

Even though Hall had become disabled in a shooting accident before the war, she became an ambulance driver in France; then she went to Great Britain and worked for the military attache in the American embassy. There she met an officer in British Special Operations and joined the French section of British intelligence. Credentialed as a stringer for the *New York Post*, she began working out of Vichy and Lyons in France. Her headquarters was her apartment, and there she trained new agents, distributed radio sets, acted as a liaison to resistance groups, and helped escaping airmen and agents.

Hall operated in France for fourteen months until the time of the North African invasion in November 1942, when she escaped across the Pyrenees to Spain and was taken back to Britain. In 1943 she was working in Madrid. Determined to return to France, she became qualified in Morse code and rejoined British intelligence. She also worked for the Office of Strategic Services (OSS). On March 21, 1944, an Allied torpedo boat deposited her on the French coast. Using the code name of DIANE, Hall organized guerrilla groups, posing as a milk maid,havinglearned to milk on her parent's summer farm in Maryland. She was the radio operator for her group of farm workers whom she directed to receive air drops. In July, she moved to the Haute Loire region and began working there with five maquis groups. She planned guerrilla operations under which four bridges and one key railroad were blown up, trains were derailed and phone lines cut. Her groups ultimately merged with the professional armies that had entered the area.

Virginia Hall is the only American woman in World War II to have received the Distinguished Service Cross, as well as the Military Order of the British Empire. Her citation read, in part,

"Continually at the risk of capture [she] directed warfare against enemy troops, installations, and communications." She later became one of the early women members of the U.S. Central Intelligence Agency (CIA).

Another notable American woman is Devereaux Rochester, who was born in New York City in 1917, also to a wealthy family. She was educated in England. When France fell, she was in Paris and escaped to Britain where she joined British Special Operations. She was given commando training in Scotland and in October 1943 was sent to France. Here she began working as a courier. In January 1944, she carried out a sabotage assignment, blowing up three train engines. In March she was ordered back to London, since officials feared the Gestapo was close on her trail. Enroute to Paris she was arrested and sent to prison at the Vittel Spa, from which the women were liberated in the autumn of 1944. Rochester achieved a remarkable record of successfully evading the Germans for almost four years. For her work, she was awarded the French Croix de Guerre and the Legion of Honor.

Virginia Roush was born in 1910 in Ohio. At the age of twenty-seven she married Philippe D'Albert Lake, a young aristocrat whom she had met while traveling in France. As a member of the French army, he was demobilized after the fall of France. The couple found themselves living in Paris, and they also owned a small house about twenty-four miles northwest of the city. Having met some escaping American pilots, the Lakes decided to join the resistance. In December 1943, Philippe was put in touch with a British agent who was trying to reestablish the Comet escape line and set up another one. Eventually, Philippe headed the Comet line, and Virginia acted as his assistant, setting up safehouses and guiding escapees. As the Normandy invasion approached, the Allied bombing campaign damaged rail lines to such an extent that it became difficult to escort airmen by train to the coast. A camp in the Freteval forest was therefore set up for evaders and Philippe and Virginia helped collect supplies.

On D Day, the Lakes had eleven airmen in their apartment in Paris whom they had to move to the camp. The only train line did not reach the camp, and no vehicles were available. The escapees set off on the 54-mile trek from the last rail station. Virginia and

Philippe bicycled from Paris and rendezvoused with them. With eighteen miles to go, seven of the men had such badly blistered feet that they could no longer continue. Virginia contacted agents in the area and was able to obtain a cart.

Virginia and an airman known as Al bicycled in front of the cart, which held the other six men and another guide. Within a short distance of the camp, Virginia and Al were stopped by German agents. Virginia's papers showed that she was an American citizen; and Al's nationality was soon discovered. Both were arrested. Roush held out during seven weeks of interrogation. She was sent to Ravensbruck and to two other concentration camps where she spent nine months. In April 1945, she was finally released. In August 1944, records show that 152 airmen had been hiding in the Freteval camp. For her work, Virginia Roush received the French Croix de Guerre and Medal of the Resistance, the Belgian Medal of King Leopold, the Order of the British Empire and the United States Medal of Freedom with Bronze Palm.

Three other women received Medals of Freedom for their work with the French resistance. Dorothy Blackman Tartiere was born in Wisconsin in 1903 and grew up on a ranch in Mexico. She married a French citizen, who was killed in the French army. As a member of the resistance, she farmed eight acres at a villa outside Paris and delivered food to evaders hiding in the city. She also assisted escapees and housed ten of them. Rosemary Wright Maeght was born in Massachusetts in 1915. She also married a Frenchman, and they inherited her mother's villa in the town of Pau, a spa center in the Pyrenees mountains. Maeght became the sector head for the Burgundy escape line, in which role she organized and funded safehouses, collected supplies and directed escape operations. She is credited with having helped ninety aviators.

Countess Roberta de Mauduit, nee Laurie, was the wife of a French aristocrat and lived in a large, 40-room chateau in Brittany which was ideal for hiding airmen. She became involved in the resistance through a French agent who had asked her to hide him. Soon she was harboring airmen. She was ultimately arrested and confined at Ravensbruck and other camps for two years. During part of this period she worked in a munitions factory that was subject to Allied bombings. She received the Medal of Freedom with Bronze Palm.

These women are among those whose exploits are detailed in Margaret Rossiter's book *Women in the Resistance*. Rossiter mentions other American women who helped them. It is not known whether there are any others who were as highly decorated as these. Rossiter points out that all of these women had the chance to leave France, but did not, and instead risked their lives to aid the Allied cause.

Resistance members were not the only American women who worked for U.S. intelligence. WACs and Women Marines worked for the OSS and other intelligence groups. In Algeria, Warrant Officer Rachel Griese sifted and winnowed out thousands of intelligence items in preparing detailed reports on German movements, strength, and defenses in southern France. Within the OSS, military and civilian women comprised twelve percent of the personnel and received thirty-six medals. Griese earned the Legion of Merit.[1]

18

The Final Months in the Pacific

In May 1945, the war was still raging in the Pacific. Army and Navy nurses and WACs were still serving in the Philippines, the China-Burma-India theater, some of the Pacific Islands, and on hospital ships. The nurses were often subject to bombings and strafings. They had also been subject to disease. In the summer of 1944, a dengue fever epidemic hit Saipan, and half the nurses succumbed. Among the men, there were five disease cases for every combat casualty. From February to June 1945, nurses on Guam, Tinian, and Saipan worked in base hospitals to which patients had been evacuated by plane and hospital ship from the major battles of Iwo Jima and Okinawa. The numbers were appalling: eighteen thousand casualties in one month from Iwo

Jima, and from April to June 1945, fifty thousand wounded from Okinawa, where fifteen thousand had been killed.[1]

Because of the mobile nature of the Pacific campaigns, the Navy came to rely on hospital ships and medically equipped transports to give on-the-scene treatment and evacuation. The USS *Samaritan* arrived off Iwo Jima on D Day plus 1, took on 251 wounded and another 355 the next day, sometimes operating within a mile of the shore. There were twenty-two nurses on the ship, who "worked tirelessly" along with other surgical staff in operating rooms that were "heavy with morphine odor and with sickening emanations from other heady drugs. . . . Marines and sailors off Iwo, in every conceivable state of mutilation . . . stared at the nurses' flushed faces, as at something new and rare."[2]

During the complex amphibious operation on Okinawa, "Seven hospital ships were used . . . to evacuate wounded despite the serious threat of enemy air attack especially the massed kamikaze raids that sunk twenty-one ships and damaged forty-three others off that island." On April 2, the USS *Relief* was attacked. On April 20, the USS *Solace* was attacked. On April 28, the USS *Comfort* sustained casualties when a kamikaze plane crashed into its starboard side. The USS*Comfort* was manned by a Navy crew and Army medical personnel. Of the twenty killed, six were nurses. Said Alice Marie Miller, of the *Solace*, "During the last of the Okinawa campaign, the kamikazes came over every night. It was probably the first time I was really frightened."[3]

Other women forced to deal with the casualties at Iwo Jima were Women Marines stationed in the casualty section at the Pentagon. Their sad, thankless task was to compose letters to widows who wrote asking how their husbands had died. The women worked with huge volumes which contained sample paragraphs because little information was allowed to be given. After researching a marine's service record and consulting the books, Neva Vredevoogd said, "we tried very hard (often with tears running down our faces) to write a letter which would get by the censors and still be kind."[4]

Army nurses in China experienced other kinds of problems, mostly with their Chinese patients. These patients often refused to follow orders given by a woman or wouldn't take medications.

They decided they had to get their own food, so "They wandered off to the bazaar in their pajamas to haggle over fresh vegetables and live ducks and chickens, which they brought back to the wards and kept under their beds." Quarantined patients also refused to stay put and often spread contagious diseases.[5]

Flight nurses were active in the Pacific. On March 6, 1945, Navy Ensign Jane Kendeigh was one of twelve flight nurses in C-47 aircraft forced to circle for eighty minutes over Iwo Jima until American artillermen ended their barrage and the planes could land. Some of the patients greeted Kendeigh's arrival with whistles and cheers; others were too badly wounded to oblige. Her plane was loaded with seventeen wounded, then flew out under fire. She later said the only incident on the otherwise uneventful flight was when a mental case decided he wanted to pilot the plane and she and the corpsman had to strap him into his litter. Of her very first flight, she said she was "not scared a bit." Kendeigh was later the first flight nurse into Okinawa.[6]

In August 1944, Second Lieutenant Kathleen Dial of Florence, Alabama was awarded the Distinguished Flying Cross, the Air Medal, and a Purple Heart for a mission in New Guinea. Dial's unit worked from four a.m. until nine p.m. every other day and went in with the second combat assault wave. On her June flight, Dial was evacuating eighteen mental patients from the front lines when her plane crash-landed on a beach (and seven men were killed upon impact.) Dial went through the plane door, broke her hip, dislocated her shoulder, and suffered a concussion. In spite of these injuries, she directed the removal of her patients until she collapsed.[7]

In early 1945, *Life* magazine correspondent Shelley Mydans visited a group of flight nurses on Saipan. In thirteen months, the one hundred serving in the Pacific had evacuated thirty-seven thousand sick and wounded and had only lost one man en route. Prior to leaving on the night flight, Mydans chatted with several of the women in their Quonset hut. Mary Creel, twenty-three, considered herself the "most crashed" flight nurse, since she had survived three crashes in three months. She figured she was living on borrowed time. Sally Jones laughed about the time her plane was forced down on Eniwetok Island. There, the soldiers were so surprised to see a woman that they "couldn't close their mouths for the usual whistle."

Soon it was time to board Lieutenant Vicki Pavlowski's flight. Mydans described an olive drab plane, men with weary faces wrapped in blankets, the smell of old bandages, blankets, and canvas. Two hours up on their eight hour flight, the cabin was cold; Vicki had not sat down and often leaned over to speak to one of the patients, most of whom quietly lay in their litters and intermittently watched her move about. Then:

> Suddenly the plane dipped and dropped. The two engines on the port side had cut out and the other two were roaring angrily in a rising pitch. I braced myself and looked at Vicki. The patients were all looking at her, too, looking for reassurance. She stood, feet apart, hanging on to the litter nearest her, steadying herself in the reeling plane. Her face had not changed and she bent down, still grasping the litter, and spoke to the boy in the tier below. He was the boy with a body cast, encased in white plaster from his waist down to his toes. She smiled at him and the patients watching her face smiled, too.
>
> The two engines cut in again, coughing and choking, and the plane steadied. I looked again at the boy across the plane . . . I tried to smile as Vicki had done but in my mind was the phrase 'prepare to ditch' and the picture of a man swimming for his life in a body cast.

With the plane flying smoothly again, Mydans lay back and thought about the other nurses she had met. She remembered Stella Hawkins' story. Her plane had crash-landed amid coconut trees on an island south of Guadalcanal. The neck of one patient was slit, and Hawkins siphoned out the blood and mucus with an ear syringe. A small boat arrived and she helped load the men. With the last on board, there was no room for her, so she swam out to the rescue ship which was lying out past coral reefs.

As the plane neared its destination at dawn, Vicki fed the men as they woke. She was now somewhat pale, and her lipstick had worn off. She had the same sense of reassurance and was still quick to smile. "We were ready to land and Vicki strapped down the patients, folded the extra blankets neatly and went forward to comb her hair and put on make-up. It is Army regulation that flight nurses look attractive and fresh when they bring the hospital ships in to land."[8]

WAC Corporal Margaret Hastings' experience in New Guinea serves as a reminder that in war even benign activities can be life-threatening. On May 13, 1945, Hastings and twenty-two other military personnel lifted off in a C-47 for a sightseeing trip over the islands. The plane crashed on a mountainside, killing twenty, including five other WACs. The island on which the survivors found themselves was so remote that the natives had never seen Caucasians before. A rescue team parachuted in ten miles from the crash site and reached the survivors on May 25. An aerial funeral was held for the dead. They were buried on the mountain, and crosses were dropped to the site.

The group returned to the base camp June 1, having gone through "incredibly wild country." At some point an aircraft communicated with Hastings via walkie-talkie and she responded, "I am fine and enjoying it all." To get off the island finally, the group had to build an airstrip from which a glider was towed out with them aboard by a low-flying plane. Hastings arrived back in the United States in early July.[9]

The final story of the Pacific war was the liberation of the Philippines. American forces landed at Tacloban, Leyte on October 20, 1944. Here, for the first time, nurses were able to work in field hospitals right behind the front lines. Nine days after the initial landings, they had set up a hospital in a Catholic cathedral and were treating patients. The battle for Leyte incurred the highest killed-to-wounded ratio of the war, one to three. There were many casualties from kamikaze attacks on ships in the harbor. Between October and December, three thousand wounded men were evacuated to New Guinea.[10]

The WACs attached to general headquarters arrived in Leyte a month after the nurses, toward the end of November. Tokyo Rose's prediction that they would never reach the Philippines almost came true. Their planes were forced to circle the airfield and were strafed while unloading. They lived and worked in rain and mud without proper footgear. "They kept communications open at Leyte between alerts that sent them into foxholes only to return to take more messages all through the night," according to the official command history. Other WACs followed the first group during the next three months. When the move was made to Manila, on Luzon, in March 1945, six operators with the Far East Air Service Command ran the headquarters switchboard for two weeks, twenty-four hours a day, seven days a week.[11]

One of the first military objectives of the U.S. Army on entering Manila was to free the prisoners in the Santo Tomas Internment Camp. It was located on a university campus on the north side of the city and American troops entering the city from the north rushed to take it. On the night of February 3, 1945, the 2d Squadron of the 8th Cavalry used a tank to batter down the gates, and within minutes the camp containing 3,500 civilian internees and the Army and Navy nurses was in American hands. During Japanese attacks immediately thereafter, a few newly freed prisoners were killed. Internees were later told that the cavalry arrived in the nick of time, since Tokyo had issued orders for all the prisoners to be killed in February.

Meanwhile, Troop G of the 8th Cavalry continued down Quezon Boulevard to the intersection with Azcarraga Street where the Bilibid Prison was located. Machine gun fire erupted from university buildings across the street and chaos was narrowly avoided as the lead tanks tried to reverse their direction. It was the next day after more American units entered the area that the 148th Infantry broke into Bilibid and, to their surprise, found eight hundred military prisoners-of-war and 530 civilians. The internees remained there overnight, while fighting raged around them. The next day, they were evacuated, and when they returned all their meager possessions had been looted.[12]

Florence Smith operated with the Manila underground until her arrest in October 1944. At the local military station, she was questioned by the Japanese and tortured with electric shocks when she gave unsatisfactory answers. During her four months' internment, Smith spent time in three prisons, including Bilibid. She was forced to sit immobile on wooden floors for fifteen hours at a stretch. She and her fellow inmates were put on a starvation diet. To drown out the moans of other prisoners under torture, they talked about food and recipes. If a guard overheard them, he would come in and hit them over the head with his sword. During this time, Smith never revealed any information about her fellow resisters. After a farcical trial, she was sentenced to three years' hard labor and sent to a women's prison outside Manila. When she was liberated on February 10, she weighed eighty pounds.

During the spring of 1945, the internees returned to the United States and were debriefed for war crimes prosecution. Smith came home in May, stayed for a while with an aunt in Buffalo, N.Y., and in July 1945, joined the Coast Guard SPARs, still anxious to fight the Japanese. In October, she received her late husband's medals: the Distinguished Service Cross, the Distinguished Unit Badge and a Purple Heart. In November 1947, she was awarded the Medal of Freedom. The Coast Guard had previously awarded her the Pacific Theater campaign ribbon for her underground work. She was the first SPAR to receive this ribbon. Other SPARs stationed in Hawaii and Alaska were also given the ribbon.[13]

The sixty-seven Army nurses held in Santo Tomas received much publicity when they returned home to the States. All were promoted, and all received the Bronze Star. During the whole time they were imprisoned, they treated patients in the camp. Lieutenant Ann Wurts said, "We nurses were too busy at Santo Tomas to worry. It didn't get any of us down."[14]

In May 1943, Lieutenant Commander Laura Cobb, ten other Navy nurses, and three civilian nurses had volunteered to set up and staff a POW camp hospital at Los Banos. They improvised a 60-bed unit. When medicines ran low, they used herbs. The nurses and other prisoners were liberated on February 23. For their work while held in captivity by the enemy, the Army awarded them the Bronze Star, and the Navy awarded them gold stars in lieu of a second Bronze Star.[15]

At least three of the Santo Tomas internees were Red Cross workers. Thomas Wolff, the Red Cross Director in the Philippines and his wife, Caroline, emerged in fair health, but malnourished. When Marie Adams, a field worker, returned to the United States, she received a check which represented her back pay with a raise from the date of her imprisonment.[16]

19

Civilian Organizations

During the war, the American Red Cross and the United Service Organizations (USO) were active at home and overseas. Domestically, the Red Cross attended disasters and served the war effort within the United States. From 1944 to 1945, it coordinated the activities of more than 7.5 million volunteers. The volunteers made and shipped 28 million packages to Allied prisoners-of-war. One POW commented that he owed his life to these care packages, "We were never without at least some Red Cross rations, even when the German transport was in shambles." Volunteers at home also taught safety and nutrition courses, worked in hospitals, recruited nurses, and provided 13.4 million units of blood. Rubie Bond, a black mother of nine who still lives in Beloit, Wisconsin, taught a home nursing class: "You could help people who needed assistance in the home and taking care of the ill . . . because of a shortage of doctors."[1]

The Red Cross also sent men and women welfare, recreation, and canteen workers overseas. They dispensed coffee and donuts in forward areas and provided recreation for the troops. Margaret Kelk served in New Caledonia, Guadalcanal, and Hawaii. She taught reading to illiterate soldiers, organized recreation activities, and worked in canteens. Her canteen work was done at Hickam Field in Hawaii. She worked the night shift with the canteen set up on the runway. "I remember slicing pineapple all night long and making coffee all night long . . .They were so happy to see American [women], to have this before they had to go in and find their unit."

Kelk also recalled one of the Santo Tomas internees she put up for the night on her return trip to the States, who told her, "We in America will never ever know what trouble is. When the Philippine [people] kill their own children to keep them from being captured by the Japanese--that's what I saw." Said Kelk, "Oh, I'll never forget that. I get emotional, too, to this day."[2]

Red Cross workers were also decorated. On April 11, 1945, the chief of staff of the Philippine Army awarded eighteen Red Cross workers, including at least one woman, the Philippine Liberation Ribbon for the assistance given to the people of Manila.[3] Mrs. Margaret Emerson received the Medal of Freedom in 1948 for her Red Cross work on Guam and Saipan.[4] Some workers were killed. In August 1944, Esther Richards was awarded a Purple Heart, posthumously. She had died at Anzio.[5]

The USO served as the home away from home for soldiers and sailors in the United States and overseas. In larger cities, centers provided food, recreation, shower facilities, and travel information. USO personnel visited hospitals, took GIs on tours, and worked in canteens. The organization was most famous for sponsoring entertainment for the troops. The comedian Bob Hope was the king of the entertainers. By the end of the war, hundreds of movie stars, singers, dancers, and musicians had put on 428,520 shows for military personnel in all corners of the world.[6]

The actress and comedian Martha Raye became best known for her "trooping." The 1944 movie, *Four Girls in a Jeep* was based on her tours of English and North African bases. Raye entertained troops in three wars. In 1969, the Academy of Motion Picture Arts and Sciences presented her with the Jean Hersholt Humanitarian Award. President George Bush awarded her the Presidential Medal of Freedom in 1993. When Raye died in October 1994, she was buried with military honors.[7]

These entertainers also took their risks. The actress Carol Lombard, a.k.a. Mrs. Clark Gable, was killed when her plane crashed into a mountainside near Las Vegas, Nevada in January 1942. She, her mother, twelve American pilots, and seven others had been en route to Los Angeles. Lombard and her mother were returning from her home state of Indiana, where they had been participating in a war bond campaign.[8]

Private news organizations worked with the military services to bring news home from the battlefronts. Many women reporters were active correspondents. Margaret Bourke-White was famous as a *Life* photographer. Born in 1904 in New York City, she graduated from Cornell University in 1927 and began her photographic career specializing in architectural and industrial subjects. In 1929, she joined the staff of the new *Fortune* magazine, then switched to the fledgling *Life* in 1935. She married writer Erskine Caldwell, and in 1941 they were together in Moscow during Hitler's invasion of Russia. At the time, Bourke-White was the only foreign photographer in the capital.

Once the United States entered the war, she was credentialed by both the Army Air Forces and *Life* magazine and journeyed first to England and then North Africa. Her ship was torpedoed on the way. In January 1943, she accompanied an air raid on an airfield in Tunisia. She continued on with American forces into the Cassino valley in Italy, and with General George S. Patton's army along the Rhine. She later photographed the death camps in Germany.[9]

Georgette "Dickey" Meyer Chapelle was another woman photographer, who competed with Bourke-White. Born in Wisconsin in 1918, she took an early interest in aviation, learned to fly, and later wrote books on women in aviation and government. During the war, she worked for *Look* magazine and began photographing and writing on women at work on the homefront. Her photographs of wounded soldiers on hospital ships coming home from the Pacific received major attention. During her career, Chapelle covered revolutions and combat in such far-flung places as Korea, Cuba, the Dominican Republic, Algeria, Lebanon, Kashmir and Vietnam. In November 1965, Chapelle accompanied a Marine patrol advancing on a Viet Cong village. A booby trap exploded, cutting down Dickey Chapelle, the first American woman correspondent ever to die in action.[10]

Other women reporters overcame considerable resistance and covered World War II as full-fledged correspondents. Their dispatches were right on the mark and widely read. Among them were Ann Stringer of the United Press, Martha Gellhorn of *Collier's*, Sonia Tomara of the *New York Herald Tribune*, Peggy Hull Deuell of the *Cleveland Plain Dealer*, and Helen Kirkpatrick of the *Chicago Daily News*.[11]

20

At Work on
the Home Front

As Americans overseas went through hardships, they were aware of support from their families at home. American women on the home front were employed in defense industries and replaced men in other jobs. They volunteered for war charities, looked after neighbors' children, and coped with rationed food, gas, tires, and absence of nylon.

The classic image of women working on the home front is that of Rosie the Riveter, producing ships, planes, tanks, and guns for the armed forces. There were women in the factories, yet the proportion of women factory workers increased from two in ten before the war only to three in ten during the war. Most women who worked were employed in administrative jobs. Rosie is still important for two reasons. First, she represented a 50 percent increase in women in the nontraditional trades, and she changed female stereotypes. Secondly, the ships, planes, and other armaments the women and men produced during the war were generally very well made. It was probably not far from the minds of many women that their husbands, fathers, or sons could be flying or sailing the planes and ships they were building.[1]

The women often worked ten to fourteen hour days in cold, unhealthy conditions. Lucille Kolkin worked in the Brooklyn Navy Yard, as the first woman shipfitter. Recalling her work Kolkin said, "We were on for fourteen hours a day, fifty-eight hours a week, eight hours on Sundays in these big, drafty shops. The sides of the shop opened up via barn-sized doors to allow us to do the very big jobs, and there were holes cut out in the floors to hold whatever part of the ship we were working on in place. Cold air rushed through these holes in the wintertime . . . and rats wandered in occasionally as well. I tell you it was a very romantic job."[2]

Rose Kaminski of Milwaukee, Wisconsin went to work for the Harnischfeger Corporation in 1944. The company made car frames for excavators, earth movers, and government tractors. Kaminski worked as a crane operator lifting frames that weighed tons. "You'd pick them up and you'd turn them and I would be just scared sick and the fellows would say, 'Don't do anything unless we give you a signal. You'll do it, you'll do fine' . . . and I learned how to move all this equipment." Kaminski worked in smoke that was so thick from welding equipment they had to open the skylights. Fires in oil drums placed on the floor to keep workers warm added to the smoke. In the wintertime, Kaminski always wore a snowsuit and boots.[3]

Many minority group women worked in nontraditional trades. The Kaiser Company's Richmond Shipyard No. 1 in California employed one thousand black women, out of six thousand black workers. They constructed Liberty ships, the well-known supply and troop ships built in quantities during the war. Eighteen of these ships were named for African-Americans, such as Harriet Tubman who escorted slaves to freedom on the underground railroad before the Civil War. Marian Anderson, the opera singer, christened the ship the *Booker T. Washington*, named for the famous black educator.[4]

Approximately 12,000 Native American women worked in manufacturing and in war related charities. They were employed in aircraft assembly plants as welders and as mechanics. They staffed fire lookout stations and worked as livestock tenders, seamstresses, and lumberjacks.

Hispanic women worked in steel, ammunition, and meat packing plants. Often living near railroads not far from their families, they repaired tracks and loaded boxcars in all kinds of weather, and cleared tracks of snow.[5]

Women worked fulltime and parttime in paid work or as volunteers in food production. They grew victory gardens, worked in canning factories, served as harvesters in the land army and ran farms and ranches. Even Girl Scouts collected milkweed for use in life preservers.

Nurses working on the home front relieved the labor shortage in hospitals. One anecdote from this author's family suggests that the war brought subtle changes on the domestic scene. My mother, then Juanita Worden Pape, and her first husband both grew up in a small Illinois farm community. She became a registered nurse, and he entered the Navy. While Dick Pape was stationed at Elizabeth City, North Carolina, my mother worked at the local hospital. At the time, African-Americans did not receive equal treatment when admitted to the emergency room--they were the last on line. My mother told me that when she was the nurse in charge, she saw to it that everyone was treated according to order of arrival and need.

When disasters and war-related accidents occurred on the home front during the war, women helped give relief. In 1943, more than five hundred Coast Guard personnel rescued seven thousand people, 25,000 livestock and over 20,000 poultry from Mississippi flood waters near St. Louis. In the 11th Naval District, twelve SPARs received a headquarters commendation for treating victims at a serious harbor fire. A hurricane hit the New Jersey coast and SPAR radio watch standers maintained their posts until waters reached their ankles. Others responded to a Cleveland gas company fire and ship and storm emergencies in Massachusetts.

Women Civil Air Patrol pilots flew disaster, search and rescue, and forest fire patrols. In the northern states, women took over from their husbands in fire watch towers and as volunteer forest fire fighters.[6]

Although only the SPARs have written their extracurricular war activities into their history, other service women at home and overseas also served as volunteers. They gave blood, helped sell war bonds, collected clothing and paper for salvage, and worked in hospitals. Choral groups were organized in every district, as were athletic teams. SPARs formed drum and bugle corps and drill teams and played in the SPARs band. A Seattle group organized a Mounted Drill Team, which appeared at horse shows. To help relieve the civilian labor shortage, they worked part-time as switchboard operators, drivers, postal clerks, baby sitters, cannery help, and harvesters on farms.[7]

From top left to right: Sylvia Honigman Everett, welder; Ida Pollack, welder; Lucille Gerwitz Kolkin, first woman ship fitter; Kitty (last name unknown), welder. These shipbuilders were on a lunch break at the Brooklin Navy Yard, circa 1943. Ida Pollack, NY.

21

Allied Women

Although this book is about American women, it is worth relating
some of the work of the women in the other Allied countries. Their
activities affected American women. They saved the lives of untold
numbers of American military personnel, through their direct action
or indirectly by harassing and targeting the enemy. They also
served as examples to both American men and women.

Conversely, what American women did to support the war
mattered to European women and sustained hope for them. In
February of 1943, the 10,000 women members of the Greek
Resistance appealed to Allied women to increase their war efforts
in a letter smuggled out by boat to Cairo. It read in part, "Thousand
of our brothers and husbands have been victims of mass executions
before our very eyes. . . . Many of us have watered the tree of
liberty with our blood and many of us are rotting in jail."[1]

Throughout the war, and particularly before and after D-Day,
Allied leaders recognized the importance of the French Resistance.

The number of networks in operation has already been noted; what has not been noted is the importance and leadership of the women. Women made better guides and agents than men. They could wander freely during the day without someone wondering why they were not at work. Women could go about collecting food and clothing for escapees and be escorted by men without questions being asked. In France, women of all social classes joined the Resistance--aristocrats, peasants, and professional women. There were married women, single women, widows, and wives of POWs. Their ages ranged from teenagers to women in their seventies.

One Belgian and three French women headed large escape organizations: Andrée de Jongh founded the Comet Line; Mary Lindell, the Comtesse de Milleville founded the Marie Claire Line; Marie Louise Dissard headed the Pat Line; and Comtesse Pauline de St. Vincent headed the Marie Odile network. Women comprised twenty to seventy percent of the membership. These four escape lines alone were responsible for getting almost 800 airmen and others to Allied countries. During the course of the war, 2,000 British and Canadian and 3,000 American air crew escaped from German-occupied France after being shot down.

Marie Madeleine Fourcade headed an intelligence network of 3,000 persons located in every important city and port in France. One-sixth were women and nine percent of them died at the hands of the Germans, never revealing any information under torture. Her network provided a fifty-five foot detailed map of German defenses on the Cotentin peninsula where the D-Day landings took place, as well as information on the V-1 and V-2 rockets.[2]

In Holland, Brunita J. Gemmeke was the only woman ever awarded the Military Order of William, the equivalent of the Medal of Honor, for her resistance work. Five other women were awarded the Resistance Cross, posthumously. Although Sweden was officially neutral, not all of its citizens were. The Swedish-born actress Greta Garbo passed information, carried messages, and arranged social and business introductions for British intelligence. Her work was particularly helpful in arranging an escape route for Niels Bohr, an important Danish atomic scientist. (Germany was well on its way to developing the bomb.)[3]

During the battle for Crete in May 1941, peasant women plowed deep furrows into fields, making German aircraft crash upon landing. Georgina Anyfantis, 20, put on a uniform and shot down German planes. Mountain women helped sabotage bridges and trekked in supplies.[4]

Jewish women held in concentration camps also resisted, against overwhelming odds. Women in Auschwitz-Berkenau who worked in the munitions factory became part of an uprising plot. They squirreled away gunpowder in their clothing and passed it to male workers. Said Rose Meth who now lives in Brooklyn, "We decided, those of us who participated, that if we're going to die, at least let us die for something." The uprising began on October 7, 1944. SS guards were killed, the crematorium was blown up, and inmates fled to the woods. Within hours, however, the Germans had killed 450 men and regained control of the camp. In the following days, five women and 14 men were tortured to get information on the conspirators. None revealed any names. On January 5, four women were then hanged as an example to the other women workers. On January 18, the Germans evacuated Auschwitz with the advance of Allied troops. During the war, there were other uprisings at Sobibor, Treblinka, and Belzen camps. Although these futile efforts seem unimportant to the war effort, they weren't. Even the threat of uprising kept German manpower tied down in camps as guards.[5]

Hannah Senesh today is considered a hero in Israel. She was born in 1921 in Budapest, Hungary. At age 18, she left for Palestine and attended school there for two years. Later, she went to live on a kibbutz. She was recruited by British intelligence which was seeking agents who could speak central European languages and would be willing to gather information and help escaping airmen. In January 1944, she left for training in Egypt. Her unit was dropped into Yugoslavia and walked two hundred miles to reach the Hungarian border. Shortly after crossing, her guides were arrested and local villagers betrayed Senesh. She was taken to Budapest for interrogation. Senesh held up under torture but was finally executed by a firing squad in November 1944.[6]

Allied women pilots were also active. A Chilean, Margot Duhalde, and three Polish women, Jadwiga Pilsudska, Anna Leska, and Barbara Wojtulanis became pilots for Britain's Air Transport

Auxiliary. So did Helen Harrison, a Canadian. In 1947, Maryse Bastie, a pre-war flight record-holder, became the first woman to be named a commander of the French Legion of Honor. In 1940, she was wounded during "military air service" (not specified). She joined the Resistance and aided the Allies even while in prison. After release, she resumed her flying and was again wounded. Her Legion of Honor award included the croix de guerre with palm.[7]

In February 1942, Nicaraguan nurses organized a parachute corps similar to the California group. There had been instances where pilots had had to bail out in mountainous areas, immediately accessible only by parachute. As a result, the government authorized the formation of the corps. Members were to make jumps in to treat injured airmen. During celebrations marking President Roosevelt's birthday, two nurses gave a parachuting demonstration for Nicaraguan President Anastacio Somoza.[8]

Of course, hundreds of thousands of women in Allied countries also joined their armed forces. Soviet women served in every branch of their military--in infantry, in armor, in transportation. They also organized three regiments of the women combat pilots: the 586th Fighter Air Regiment, the 587th Bomber Regiment, and the 588th Night Bomber Regiment. Members of the 588th bomber group flew 24,000 missions and 23 women became Heroes of the Soviet Union. Lily Litvak and Katya Budanova flew with men's units and became fighter pilot aces. Russian women worked behind German lines as partisan fighters. Ludmilla Pavlichenco is credited with 309 personal kills.[9]

Unlike American women, British women were drafted. They also worked at jobs American women did not. Ambulance drivers were among the most heroic women in Britain. Lady Edwina Mountbatten, wife of Lord Louis, who was later Supreme Allied Commander in Southeast Asia, headed the St. John's Ambulance Brigade in London. Night after night, she drove to bombing sites. One biographer described a night in November 1940:

From St. Mary's they drove down to the Watney Street Shelter, under the railway station. The raid had reached one of its peaks. Bombs were falling all round them, and on the way over the car was hit again and again by falling debris.

"I think we'd better take cover till it eases off a bit," Sticher [the superintendent] suggested.

"No," [Mountbatten] said quietly, "Let's get on with the job."[10]

At Dunkirk, British army women, as well as men, were evacuated. As an army subaltern, Mary Churchill, Winston Churchill's daughter, manned an antiaircraft battery and served as her father's aide-de-camp at the Quebec conference with Roosevelt in 1943. Members of the Women's Royal Naval Service served on troops transports as crew members. They taught naval tactics to officers. They became coxswains and crews on launches and boats that ferried personnel, dispatches, and supplies. At D-Day, some served as harbor pilots. One crew towed in a ship disabled during the invasion.[11]

British intelligence radio operators and agents were dropped into France to work with resistance groups. Noor Inayat Khan, code-named "Madeleine," refused to abandon her post in Paris after the rest of her network had been arrested and then she, too, was detained. She was chained for ten months in a squatting position and sent to a concentration camp and shot. She was awarded the George Cross and the croix de guerre, posthumously.[12]

The activities of these Allied women also serve as a standard against which to measure those of the Americans. What becomes clear is that much of what women do, and are expected to do in war is determined by need. The Europeans were fighting a mad regime intent upon enslaving and exterminating whole populations. Their women were allowed to function in more non-traditonal roles and made more sacrifices because there was no choice. Even though America suffered huge casualties in World War II, 963,000 killed and wounded, it was never necessary to put the lives of great numbers of women (i.e., compared to the men's) at risk, and the national territory remained secure. So, in the final analysis, the definition of gender roles is very dependent upon circumstance and volition. In war, ordinary people are forced to do extraordinary things, and the fragility of gender definitions becomes most clear.

Navy WAVE company passes in review at Hunter College, NY,

Women Marine musicians: the only official Marine Corps
Women's Reserve Band, organized in November 1943, to
provide music for reviews and concerts. Camp Le Jeune, N.C.,
June 1944. U.S. Marine Corps.

22

Conclusion

In August 1945, members of the Marine Corps Women's Reserve band were told by their commanding officer that Japan was expected to surrender at any time, and that they had to be ready to fall out and parade on a moment's notice. Word came at approximately 1900 hours on August 14. For three hours, the band marched and played every song by heart because in the confusion of celebration, members were unable to read their sheet music. The women played "until their lips were sore, and blisters formed on their fingers and heels. . . . And, when entire sections couldn't play because of their tears, the drums just beat out the cadence."[1]

By the end of World War II, 350,000 American women had served in the armed forces and hundreds of thousands more had worked on the home front and overseas as civilians. The women who volunteered served their country proudly. They also helped to earn women a permanent place in the American military establishment. The military nurses made an immeasurable contribution. Over thirty percent of the registered nurses in the United States served in the armed forces. Two hundred and one were killed which is a small number compared to the men's casualties; however, the number of dead is not a full indication of service.

Toward the end of the war, a severe nursing shortage existed. In his State of the Union address in January 1945, President Franklin Roosevelt stated that there were 42,000 Army nurses then in service, and 18,000 more were needed. An additional 2,000 were required by the Navy:

> The present shortage of Army nurses is reflected in undue strain on the existing force. More than a thousand nurses are now hospitalized and part of this is due to overwork. The shortage is also indicated by the fact that eleven Army hospital units have been sent overseas without their complement of nurses. . . . It is tragic that the gallant women who have volunteered for service as nurses should be so overworked. It is tragic that our wounded men should ever want for the best possible nursing care.

Roosevelt went on to urge amending the Selective Service Act to draft nurses. By April 1945, such a bill had passed the House of Representatives and been reported out of the Senate Military Affairs Committee. The effect of V-E Day in May, however, was to abort its passage.[2]

The work and bravery of the women were recognized by the military. In the Army Nurse Corps, 1,619 medals and commendations were awarded, which included the Distinguished Service Medal, the Silver Star, the Distinguished Flying Cross, the Soldier's Medal, the Bronze Star, the Air Medal, the Legion of Merit, the Army Commendation Medal, and the Purple Heart. Sixteen medals were awarded posthumously, because of death from enemy action. In the Women's Army Corps, 657 received medals and commendations, including the Distinguished Service Medal, the Legion of Merit, the Air Medal, the Soldier's Medal, the Bronze Star, and the Purple Heart.

For her leadership and renowned administration skills, Mildred McAfee was awarded the Distinguished Service Medal. Among Navy nurses, the Legion of Merit went to Ann Bernatitus for her work on Bataan and Corregidor. Besides the Cobb group, two other Navy nurses received Bronze Stars, and 42 received commendations. Four were killed in plane crashes.

Col. Ruth Streeter was awarded the Legion of Merit. In November 1988, the headquarters building of the Fourth Recruit Training Battalion on Parris Island was named in her honor.

For her leadership, Dr. Dorothy Stratton received the Legion of Merit. Other ranking SPAR officers received the Secretary of the Navy's Commendation. One SPAR was awarded a Silver Life-Saving Medal for rescuing a fellow member from drowning.[3]

Memorials were dedicated to other women service members. One Army hospital, a Red Cross facility, and a church window, as well as a community center, nurses' quarters, and a library at three private hospitals were named after World War II nurses. Lt. Frances Slanger, ANC, who was killed by shelling on October 21, 1944, was honored when her name was given to both a hospital ship and a P-38 aircraft. The Women's Club of Dallas County, Alabama, raised funds and purchased a bomber for the Army Air Forces. They named it after Kitty Driskell Barber, a nurse who was killed in a plane crash in the Mediterranean. The gravesite of Second Lt. Louise W. Bosworth, ANC, in Hamm, Luxembourg, was adopted by the National Association of Nurses in Luxembourg, as a tribute to the American nurses who served there.[4]

On November 10, 1943, in New Orleans, the statue nicknamed "Molly Marine" was dedicated to honor all female members of the· Marine Corps. In 1950, a dormitory on the Louisiana State University campus was named after Germaine Laville, an aerial gunnery instructor who, along with another female and three males died in a building fire at the Marine Corps Air Station in Cherry Point, North Carolina. She was one of a total of eighteen Women Marines who died on duty.[5]

On June 12, 1944, the U.S. Coast Guard Cutter *Spar* was commissioned in honor of the Coast Guard women. Today, it is still on active duty as a buoy tender and homeported in South Portland, Maine. In February 1995, a new administration building at Coast Guard Base Honolulu was named after SPAR Florence Smith Finch.[6]

Combat ships had also been named for women. The troop transport *Susan B. Anthony* participated in the D-Day invasion. Unfortunately, at 8:20 a.m., on June 7, 1944, it hit a mine on its approach to Omaha Beach and sank quickly. In August 1944, the Navy announced the construction of a destroyer, its only combatant ship to honor a woman. It was to be named for Mrs. Lenah S. Higbee, the first Superintendent of the Navy Nurse Corps and a winner of the Navy Cross. The Coast Guard cutter *Harriet Lane* was the second one to be named after President James Buchanan's niece. The first had had a notable career during the Civil War.[7]

Military officers had personal praise for the women. Gen. Douglas MacArthur said the WACs were "my best soldiers, because they worked harder than men, seldom complained, and were well-disciplined troops." Chief of Naval Operations Adm. Ernest King issued a report in April 1944, which complimented the women under his command in the Navy, Marines, and Coast Guard:

> As a result of their competence, their hard work and their enthusiasm, the release of men for sea duty has been accompanied in many cases, particularly in offices, by increases in efficiency . . . and it is a pleasure to report that, in addition to their having earned an excellent reputation as part of the Navy, they have become an inspiration to all in naval uniform.[8]

Perhaps the best testimony came from the soldiers themselves. In early October 1944, two weeks before she died, Lt. Slanger of the Army Nurse Corps was one of a group of nurses who wrote a letter to the Army newspaper, *Stars and Stripes*, which read in part, "Sure we rough it. But compared to the way you men are taking it we can't complain nor do we feel that bouquets are due us . . . it is to you we doff our helmets."

Hundreds of soldiers replied and one wrote, "To all Army nurses overseas: We men were not given the choice of working in the battlefield or the home front . . . We are here because we have to be. You are here because you felt you were needed. So, when an injured man opens his eyes to see one of you . . . concerned with his welfare, he can't but be overcome by the very thought that you are doing it because you want to . . . you endure whatever hardships you must to be where you can do us the most good."⁹

After twelve long hours of work, 2nd Lt. Nancy N. Gorton finds time to write a letter home, by the light of a candle in her quarters somewhere in France. Evacuation Hospital. U.S. Army, Center of Military History

APPENDIX

Description of U.S. Army, Navy, and Civilian Decorations and Ribbons Awarded to American Women in Order of Precedence*

MILITARY DECORATIONS AND RIBBONS

Distinguished Service Cross (equivalent, Navy Cross)
Any person serving with the Army of the United States who distinguishes himself by extraordinary heroism in connection with military operations against an armed enemy. It is awarded only for combat service.

Distinguished Service Medal
Any person who, while serving in any capacity with the Army or Navy of the United States since 6 April 1917, shall have distinguished himself by exceptionally meritorious service to the Government in a duty of great responsibility. It is awarded for combat or non-combat service.

Silver Star
Any person who, while serving in any capacity with the Army or Navy of the United States since 6 December 1941, shall have distinguished himself conspicuously by gallantry and intrepidity in action, not sufficient to justify the award of the Medal of Honor or the Distinguished Service or Navy Cross....It is awarded for combat service only.

Legion of Merit
Personnel of the armed forces of the United States and the Philippines; and personnel of the armed forces of friendly foreign nations who, since 8 September 1939, shall have distinguished themselves by exceptionally meritorious conduct in the

performance of outstanding services. It is awarded for combat or non-combat services.

Distinguished Flying Cross

Any person who, while serving in any capacity with the Air Corps of the Army, National Guard, and Organized Reserves, or with United States Navy, Marine Corps, or Coast Guard, subsequent to 6 April 1917, has distinguished himself by heroism or extraordinary achievement while participating in an aerial flight. Also members of military, naval, or air forces of foreign governments, while serving with the United States. It is awarded for combat or non-combat services.

Soldier's Medal (equivalent, Navy and Marine Corps Medal)

Any person who, while serving in any capacity with the United States Army, National Guard or Organized Reserves, shall have distinguished himself or herself by heroism not involving actual conflict with an armed enemy. The act of heroism must have meant personal hazard or danger and the voluntary risk of life. It is awarded for non-combat services only.

Bronze Star

Any person who, while serving in any capacity in or with the Army, Navy, Marine Corps or Coast Guard of the United States on or after 7 December 1941, distinguishes, or has distinguished himself, by heroic or meritorious achievement or service, not involving participation in aerial flight in connection with military or naval operations against an enemy of the United States....The Bronze Star Medal may be awarded to recognize minor acts of heroism in actual combat or single acts of merit, or meritorious service either in sustained operational activities against an enemy or in direct support of such operations. It is awarded for combat service only.

Air Medal

Any person who, while serving in any capacity in or with Army, Navy, Marine Corps or Coast Guard of the United States subsequent to 8 September 1939, distinguishes or has distinguished

124

himself by meritorious achievement while participating in an aerial flight. It is awarded for combat or non-combat service.

Army Commendation Ribbon
Originally only a ribbon authorized in 1945. Medal was authorized in 1949. Given to any member of the armed forces of the United States who, while serving in any capacity with the Army shall have distinguished himself, either in combat or non-combat action, by meritorious achievement or meritorious service.

Navy Commendation Ribbon
Any person of the Navy, Marine Corps, and Coast Guard who have [sic] received an individual letter of commendation signed by the Secretary of the Navy, the Commander in Chief, United States Fleet, the Commander in Chief, United States Pacific Fleet, or the Commander in Chief, the United States Atlantic Fleet for an act of heroism or service performed between 6 December 1941, and 11 January 1944. . . . It is awarded for combat or non-combat service.

Purple Heart
Persons wounded in action against the enemy of the United States while serving with the Army, Navy, Marine Corps, or Coast Guard of the United States or as result of act of such enemy, if wound necessitated treatment by a medical officer. Also to next of kin of persons killed in action. It is awarded for combat service only.

CIVILIAN MEDALS

Medal of Freedom
The Medal of Freedom created by Executive Order No. 9586 of 6 July 1945 may be awarded to any person, other than a member of the Armed Forces who, on or after 7 December 1941, shall have performed a meritorious act or service which (a) aided the United States in the prosecution of a war against an enemy or enemies (b) aided any nation engaged with the United States in the prosecution of a war against a common enemy or enemies...and for which act

or service the award of any other federal decoration is considered inappropriate.

This medal is awarded to citizens and members of the armed forces of foreign nations in four degrees, corresponding to certain American military decorations. Three are in the form of palms to be worn on the suspension ribbon. They are: Gold Palm (equivalent to the Legion of Merit, Chief Commander); Silver Palm (Legion of Merit, Commander); Bronze Palm (Legion of Merit, Officer and Legionnaire); without Palm (Bronze Star Medal). Citizens of the United States are awarded this medal only without Palm.

*Silver Life-Saving Medal***

Life-Saving Medals may be awarded to any person who rescues or endeavors to rescue any other person from drowning, shipwreck or other peril of the water. In order for a person to be eligible for a Life-Saving Medal the rescue or attempted rescue must take place in waters within the United States or subject to the jurisdiction thereof. . . . If such rescue or attempted rescue is made at the risk of one's own life and evidences extreme and heroic daring, the medal shall be of gold. If such rescue or attempted rescue is not sufficiently distinguished to deserve the medal of gold but evidences the exercise of such signal exertion as to merit recognition, the medal shall be of silver. Life-Saving Medals may be awarded posthumously.

* Descriptions taken from 1954, *U.S. Navy and Marine Corps Awards Manual* [with Army citations added where applies] and *American Medals and Decorations* by Evans E. Kerrigan (Noroton, Conn.: Medallic Press, 1990). Kerrigan is quoted for the Soldier's Medal, Army Commendation, and Medal of Freedom text following the word "inappropriate." There was a 1952 edition to the Purple Heart which probably added the reference to medical treatment. In other words, a combat condition such as frost bite which must be treated by a medical officer would merit a Purple Heart.

** Life-Saving Medals are Treasury Department medals (since 1967 Transportation Department) also given to Coast Guard personnel. For similar rescues, other service members would receive the Soldier's Medal or the Navy and Marine Corps Medal.

NOTES

NOTES TO CHAPTER 1
A World at War

1. William Manchester, *The Last Lion: Winston Spencer Churchill, Alone 1932-1940* (Boston: Little Brown and Company, 1988), p. 548; Samuel Eliot Morison, *History of United States Naval Operations in World War II: The Battle of the Atlantic, September 1939 - May 1943* (Boston: Little Brown and Company, 1988), vol. 1, p. 63

2. *The New York Times Magazine*, 24 October, 1943, p. 18

3. J. H. Hunter, *Adrift: The Story of Twenty Days on a Raft in the South Atlantic* (Grand Rapids, Mich.: Zonedevan Publishing House, 1943)

4. *The New York Times*, 23 July 1941, p. 14; Doris Weatherford, *American Women and World War II* (New York: Facts on File, 1990), pp. 8-9

5. *The New York Times*, 12 October 1941, II, p.

6. *The New York Times*, 31 March 1940, p. 30

7. *The New York Times*, 26 September 1941, p. 5; Jane Goodell, *They Sent Me to Iceland* (New York: Ives Washburn, Inc., 1943), p. 46; C. Kay Larson, "The Coast Guard Auxiliary in World War II" (Paper prepared for U.S. Coast Guard Auxiliary, First Coast Guard District, Southern Region, World War II Commemoration Committee, 1994), p. 14

8. Margaret Rossiter, *Women in the Resistance* (New York: Praeger Publishers, 1986), pp. 189-199; "Strictly Feminine," *Coast Guard Magazine*, December 1943, pp. 31-32; *The New York Times*, 13 May 1942, p. 7

9. *The New York Times*, 19 June 1942, p. 3

10. Robert Erwin Johnson, *Coast Guard-Manned Naval Vessels In World War II* (Washington, D.C.: U.S. Coast Guard, 1993), p. 3; Winston S. Churchill, *The Second World War: The Hinge of Fate* (Boston: Hougton Mifflin Company, 1950), p. 81; Judith A. V. Harlan, Interview by telephone, 20 November 1994

11. *The New York Times*, 8 February 1945, p.2; United States of America, 50th Anniversary of World War II Commemoration Committee, Fact Sheet: *Women Marines in WWII* (Washington, D.C., 1994)

12. *The New York Times*, 23 May 1940, p. 18; *The New York Times*, 19 June 1940, p. 14; *The New York Times*, 7 July 1940, p. 6

13. World Wide Photo, a subsidiary of Associated Press. Captions from photo file indexed under, "U.S. Defense: Home Guards." New York, N.Y.

14. Larson, *"The Coast Guard Auxiliary in World War II,"* p. 14

NOTES TO CHAPTER 2
Pearl Harbor

1. John Costello, *The Pacific War, 1941-1945* (New York: William Morrow and Company, Quill, 1981), pp. 132-142.

2. Deborah G. Douglas, *United States Women in Aviation, 1940-1985* (Washington, D.C.: Smithsonian Institution Press, 1991), pp. 3, 45.

3 . Litoff, Judy Bennett and David C. Smith, *We're in This War, Too: World War II Letters from American Women in Uniform* (New York: Oxford University Press, 1994), pp.17-18

4. The strength figure given by both the Surgeon General and the War Department as of the end of December 1941 was 7,043, which varies from the 1,000 figure in Bellafaire. The discrepancy arises from the call up of reserve nurses which was going on continually at the time. Quoting from correspondence from the Army Nurse Historian, "These [the Surgeon General and War Dept.] figures are for both regular and reserve nurses. Since the reserve nurses were called to active duty at different times, it is not possible to say that [the] total number were on active duty." However, the number on active duty was probably much larger than 1,000, so the 7,000 figure has been used. The 10,000 increase noted in the "Directors" chapter was also provided by the Historian and conforms to the figure given by Bellafaire (Army Nurse Corps Historian to C. Kay Larson, 21 February 1995)

5. Judith A. Bellafaire, *The Army Nurse Corps,* CMH Pub. 72-14 (Washington, D.C.: Center of Military History, n.d.), pp. 3-4; Costello, *The Pacific War,* p. 140.

6. Barbara Tomlin, "Beyond Paradise: The U.S. Navy Nurse Corps in the Pacific in World War II (Part One)," *MINERVA: Quarterly Report on Women and the Military,* vol. 11, no. 2 (Summer 1993), pp. 33-38.

7. Bellafaire, *The Army Nurse Corps,* pp. 3-4, 24-29; United States of America, 50th Anniversary of World War II Commemoration Committee, Fact Sheet: *Women in World War II* (Washington, D.C., 1994); Robert V. Piemonte and Cindy Gurney, eds., *Highlights in the History of the Army Nurse Corps* (Washington, D.C.: Center of Military History, 1987), p. 13.

NOTES TO CHAPTER 3
The Philippines

1. William Manchester, *America's Caesar: Douglas MacArthur, 1880-1964.* (Boston: Little, Brown and Company, 1978) p. 248; John Costello, *The Pacific War, 1941-1945.* (New York: William Morrow and Company, 1981) pp. 212-213

2. *The U.S. Army Campaigns of World War II: Philippine Islands, December 7, 1941 - May 10, 1942,* CMH Pub 72-3 (Washington, D.C.: Center of Military History, 1992), pp, 9-12; John Costello, *The Pacific War, 1941-1945* (New York: William Morrow and Company, Quill, 1981), p. 160; R. Renton Hind, *Spirits Unbroken* (n.p., 1946), pp. 20, 239; Judith A. Bellafaire, *The Army Nurse Corps,* CMH Pub 72-14 (Washington, D.C.: Center of Military History, n.d.), pp. 4-6; Mary E.V. Frank, Army Nurse Corps Historian, "Army and Navy Nurses Held as Prisoners of War During World War II," *MINERVA: Quarterly Report on Women and the Military,* vol. 6, no. 2 (Summer 1988), pp. 82-90; Listings of Army nurse prisoners-of-war. Photocopied (Washington, D.C.: Center of Military History, Office of the Army Nurse Corps Historian); Louis Morton, *The War in the Pacific: The Fall of the Philippines,* United States Army in World War II (Washington, D.C.: Department of the Army, Office of the Chief of Military History, 1953), pp. 247, 380-381

3. William Manchester, *America's Caesar: Douglas MacArthur, 1880-1964* (Boston: Little, Brown and Company, 1988), pp. 248-271; Costello, *The Pacific War,* pp. 212-213

4. Bellafaire, *The Army Nurse Corps,* pp. 4-6; Frank, "Army and Navy Nurses,"* pp. 86-90; Costello, *The Pacific War, 1941-1945,* pp. 160, 212-213; *Philippine Islands,* pp. 1-22; Morton, *Fall of the Philippines,* p. 383

5. *The New York Times,* 28 July 1945, p. 13; *The New York Times.*8 November 1947, p. 20; *The Ithaca (N.Y.) Journal,* March 1995, p.1

NOTES TO CHAPTER 4
Wolves at the Door

1. Homer Hickam, Jr., *Torpedo Junction: U-Boat War Off America's East Coast, 1942* (Annapolis, Md.: Naval Institute Press, 1989), pp. 20, 54-65; C. Kay Larson, "The Coast Guard Auxiliary in World War II," (Paper prepared for U.S. Coast Guard Auxiliary, First Coast Guard District, Southern Region, World War II Commemoration Committee, 1994), pp. 1-4; U.S. Coast Guard, Public Information Division, *The Coast Guard at War: The Temporary Component of the Coast Guard Reserve,* vol. 20 (Washington, D.C.: U.S. Coast Guard, (January 1) 1948), p. 23

2. *The New York Times,* 22 January 1942, p. 14; *The New York Times,* 8 March 1942, III, p. 7; *The New York Times,* 6 July 1942, p. 17; *The New York Times,* 7 July 1942, p. 14

3. Larson, "The Coast Guard Auxiliary in World War II," pp. 1-16; U. S. Coast Guard Auxiliary, "With the U.S. Coast Guard Auxiliary," *Yachting,* March 1943, p. 57; Keith Spangler, PA1, USCG, "Airborne at 77," *Commandant's Bulletin,* January 1977, pp. 12-13; U.S. Coast Guard Auxiliary, 13th Naval District, *Norwester,* Annual Edition, 1945 (Seattle, Wash.: U.S. Coast Guard Auxiliary, 1945), p. 121

4. *The New York Times,* 5 February 1942, p. 18; Mary C. Stremlow, *Free a Marine to Fight: Women Marines in World War II* (Washington, D.C.: Marine Corps Headquarters, History and Museums Division, 1994) p. 4; Deborah G. Douglas, *United States Women in Aviation, 1940-1985* (Washington, D.C.: Smithsonian Institution Press, 1991), p. 4; Press file on Cecil Kenyon, Photocopied (Bethpage, N.Y.: Northrop Grumman Corp., History Center)

5. Charles P. May, *Women in Aeronautics* (New York: Thomas Nelson & Sons, 1962), p. 165

6. Larson, "The Coast Guard Auxiliary in World War II," pp. 4-5; W. W. Wilson, "Modern Conveniences Boon to Only Woman Lighthouse Keeper," *Coast Guard Magazine,* August 1945, pp. 36-37; Eleanor C. Bishop, *Prints in the Sand: The U.S. Coast Guard Beach Patrol During World War II* (Missoula, Mont.: Pictorial Histories Publishing Co., 1989), pp. 31, 57

7. *The New York Times,* 6 July 1942, p. 18; *The New York Times,* 11 March 1944, p. 17; *The New York Times,* 11 January 1944, p. 16

NOTES TO CHAPTER 5
Axis Passions, Allied Victories

1. William Stevenson, *A Man Called Intrepid* (New York: Random House, Ballantine Books, 1982), pp. 108, 341-373; David Kahn, *The Codebreakers: The Story of Secret Writing* (New York: The Macmillan Company, 1967), pp. 486-488

NOTES TO CHAPTER 6
Mobilization

1. Jeanne Holm, *Women in the Military: An Unfinished Revolution* (Novato, Cal.: Presidio Press, 1982), p. 12. In 1977 Congress recdognized the World War I telephone operators as U.S. Army veterans entitled to benefits. Dorothy and Carl J. Schneider, *Into the Breach: American Women Overseas in World War I* (New York: Viking, 1991), pp. 177-187

2. Bettie J. Morden, *The Women's Army Corps, 1945-1978* (Washington, D.C.: U.S. Army Center of Military History, 1990) pp. 3-13; U.S., *Statutes at Large*, vol. 57, pt. 1, ch. 187

3. U.S., *Statutes at Large*, vol. 56, pt. 1, ch. 538, 639, 385; vol. 58, pt. 1, ch. 428; Jean Ebbert and Marie-Beth Hall, *Crossed Currents: Navy Women from WWI to Tailhook* (Washington, D.C.: Brassey's (U.S.), 1993), p. 36

4. U.S., *Statutes at Large*, vol. 57, pt. 1, ch. 297, 378; *The Story of You in Navy Blue* (Washington, D.C.: U.S. Department of the Navy, 1944); Mary C. Stremlow, Colonel, USMCR (Ret.), *Free a Marine to Fight: Women Marines in World War II* (Washington, D.C.: Marine Corps Headquarters, History and Museums Division, 1994), p. 5; U.S. Coast Guard, Public Information Division, *The Coast Guard at War: Women's Reserve*, vol. 22 A (Washington, D.C.: U.S. Coast Guard, (April 15), 1948), p. 15

5. Doris Weatherford, *American Women and World War II* New York: Facts on File, 1990), p. 11; Mary C. Lyne and Kay Arthur, Lieutenants, USCGR(W), *Three Years Behind the Mast: The Story of the United States Coast Guard SPARS* (Washington, D.C.: n.p., 1946), p. 108

6. U.S. Department of the Army, Center of Military History, Office of the Army Nurse Corps Historian, Washington, D.C., Telephone interview, 25 August 1995

7. U.S. Coast Guard, *Women's Reserve*, p. 244; Stremlow, *Free a Marine to Fight*, p. 7

8. United States of America, 50th Anniversary of World War II Commemoration Committee, Fact Sheet: *Women in World War II* (Washington, D.C.: n.p., 1994); U.S. Coast Guard, Women's Reserve, p. 187, 205

NOTES TO CHAPTER 7
Minority Women

1. Bettie J. Morden, *The Women's Army Corps, 1945-1978* (Washington, D.C.: U. S. Army, Center of Military History, 1990), pp. 16-18

2. Deborah G. Douglas, *United States Women in Aviation, 1940-1985* (Washington, D.C.: Smithsonian Institution Press, 1991), pp. 33-34, 49-50; United States of America, 50th Anniversary of World War II Commemoration Committee. Fact Sheet: *Tuskegee Airmen* (Washington, D.C.: n.p., 1994); Darlene Clark Hine, ed., *Black Women in America: An Historical Encyclopedia*, vol. 1 (New York: Carlson Publishing, 1993), s.v., Bragg, pp. 160-161

3.Judith A. Bellafaire, *The Army Nurse Corps*, CMH Pub. 72-14 (Washington, D.C.: Center of Military History, n.d.), pp. 8-9; Commemoration Committee, Fact Sheet: *African Americans in World War II*

4. Jean Ebbert and Marie-Beth Hall, *Crossed Currents: Navy Women from WWI to Tailhook* (Washington, D.C.: Brassey's (U.S.), 1993), p. 86; Robin J. Thomson, *The Coast Guard & the Women's Reserve in World War II* (Washington, D.C.: U. S. Coast Guard, 1992), p. 5; Peter A. Soderbergh, *Women Marines: The World War II Era* (Westport, Conn.: Praeger Publishers, 1992), p. 18

5. Commemoration Committee, Fact Sheet: *Hispanic Americans*; Mattie E. Treadwell, *The Women's Army Corps*, United States Army in World War II, Special Studies (Washington, D.C.: Department of the Army, Office of the Chief of Military History, 1954), p. 435; U.S. Coast Guard, *Coast Guard Magazine*, November 1945, p. 70

6. Commemoration Committee, Fact Sheet: *Native Americans*; C. G. Salisbury, Superintendent, Ganado Mission, Ganado, Ariz. to Associated Press, 3 March 1946, correspondence contained in photo file indexed under, "U.S.: Nurses, Misc." (New York: World Wide Photo, a subsidiary of Associated Press); Michael Stevens, ed., *Voices of the Wisconsin Past: Women Remember the War, 1941-1945* (Madison, Wis.: State Historical Society of Wisconsin, 1993), pp. 58-60; Douglas, *United States Women in Aviation*, p. 49; *The New York Times*, 3 August 1943, p. 16

7. Commemoration Committee, Fact Sheet: *Asian Americans in World War II*; Treadwell, The Women's Army Corps, p. 332; Douglas, *United States Women in Aviation, 1940-1985*, p. 49-50; *The New York Times*, 3 April 1945, p. 44; *The New York Times*, 6 April 1945, p. 6

NOTES TO CHAPTER 8
The Directors

1.Jeanne Holm, *Women in the Military: An Unfinished Revolution* (Novato, Cal.: Presidio Press, 1982), p. 30; Bettie J. Morden, *The Women's Army Corps, 1945-1978* (Washington, D.C.: U.S. Army Center of Military History, 1992), p. 6; *The New York Times*, 17 August 1995, p. B13; *Who's Who im America*, 39th ed., s.v. Oveta Culp Hobby

2.Charles F. Bombard, Colonel, ANC, Wyonona M. Bice-Stephens, Major, ANC, and Karen L. Ferguson, Major, ANC, "The Soldier's Nurse: Colonel Florence A. Blanchfield," *MINERVA: Quarterly Report on Women and the Military*, vol. 6, no. 4 (Winter 1988), pp. 43-49; U.S. Department of the Navy, Library, Washington, D.C., Telephone interview, 12 December 1994

3. Jean Ebbert and Marie-Beth Hall, *Crossed Currents: Navy Women from WWI to Tailhook* (Washington, D.C.: Brassey's (U.S.), 1993), pp. 32-34; *The New York Times*, 4 September 1994, p. 41; *Who's Who in America*, 39th ed., s.v., Mildred McAfee Horton

4. Robin J. Thomson, PA2, USCG, *The Coast Guard & the Women's Reserve in World War II* (Washington, D.C.: U.S. Coast Guard, 1992), p. 1; *Who's Who in America*, 31st ed., s.v., Dorothy Constance Stratton

5. *The New York Times*, 2 October 1990, p. B6; Mary C. Stremlow, Colonel, USMCR (Ret.), *Free a Marine to Fight: Women Marines in World War II* (Washington, D.C.: Marine Corps Headquarters, History and Museums Division, 1994), p. 3

6. *The New York Times*, 2 October 1990, p. B6; Mary C. Stremlow, *Free a Marine to Fight: Women Marines in World War II* (Washington, D.C.: Marine Corps Headquarters, History and Museums Division, 1994), p. 3

7. Mattie E. Treadwell, *The Women's Army Corps, United States Army in World War II, Special Studies* (Washington, D.C.: Department of the Army, Office of the Chief of Military History, 1954), p. 414; Ebbert, *Crossed Currents*, p. 17, 32, 47, 51

8. Treadwell, *The Women's Army Corps*, p. 765, 192; Judith A. Bellafaire, *The Army Nurse Corps*, CMH Pub. 72-14 (Washington, D.C.: Center of Military History, n.d.), p.1, 6; Ebbert, *Crossed Currents*, p. 48-50, 64

9. Stremlow, *Free a Marine to Fight*, p. 7

NOTES TO CHAPTER 9
G. I. Janes

1. Bettie J. Morden, *The Women's Army Corps, 1945-1978* (Washington, D.C.: U.S. Army Center of Military History, 1990), pp. 7, 9; U.S. Coast Guard, Public Information Division, *The Coast Guard at War: Women's Reserve*, vol. 22 A (Washington, D.C.: U.S. Coast Guard, (April 15), 1948), pp. 63-69, 95-97; Mary C. Stremlow, *Free a Marine to Fight: Women Marines in World War II* (Washington, D.C.: Marine Corps Headquarters, History and Museums Division, 1994), pp. 7-15; United States of America, 50th Anniversary of World War II Commemoration Commitee, Fact Sheet: *Women in the Navy* (Washington, D.C.: n.p., 1994)

2. Marilyn Willis, Interview by telephone, 3 September 1995

3. Morden, *The Women's Army Corps*, p. 8; Stremlow, *Free a Marine to Fight*, pp. 8-11; U.S. Coast Guard, *Women's Reserve*, pp. 77, 105

4. Stremlow, *Free a Marine to Fight*, pp. 14-15; U.S. Coast Guard, *Women's Reserve*, pp. 99-101, 73; Joy Bright Hancock, *Lady in the Navy: A Personal Reminiscence.* (Annapolis, Md.: Naval Institute Press, 1972) pp. 75-149

5. Mary C. Lyne and Kay Arthur, Lieutenants, USCGR(W), *Three Years Behind the Mast: The Story of the United States Coast Guard SPARS* (Washington, D.C.: n.p., 1946.), p. 44; Jean Ebbert and Marie-Beth Hall, *Crossed Currents: Navy Women from WWI to Tailhook* (Washington, D.C.: Brassey's (U.S.), 1993), pp. 50, 62.

6. Jean Horsfall, Telephone interview, 25 November 1994; *The New York Times Magazine*, 20 June 1943, pp. 12-13.

7. W. W. Wilson, "Modern Conveniences Boon to Only Woman Lighthouse Keeper," *Coast Guard Magazine*, August 1945, pp. 36-37; *The Ithaca (N.Y.) Journal*, 6 March 1995, p. 32-33; Mattie E. Treadwell, *The Women's Army Corps*, United States Army in World War II, Special Studies (Washington, D.C.: Department of the Army, Office of the Chief of Military History, 1954), p. 381.

8. *The New York Times Magazine*, 24 October 1943, p. 18.

9. Morden, *The Women's Army Corps*, pp. 9-10; U.S. Coast Guard, *Women's Reserve*, p. 101; "Permanent WAVES," *Newsweek*, 10 August 1942, pp. 30-32; Jean Ebbert and Marie-Beth Hall, *Crossed Currents: Navy Women from WWI to Tailhook* (Washington, D.C.: Brassey's (U.S.), 1993 pp. 52-53; Mattie E. Treadwell, *The Women's Army Corps*, United States Army in World War II, Special Studies (Washington, D.C.:

Department of the Army, Office of the Chief of Military History, 1954), p. 435

10. Samuel Eliot Morison, *History of United States Naval Operations in World War II: The Invasion of France and Germany, 1944-1945*, vol. 11 (Boston: Little Brown and Company, 1988), p. 77

11. Treadwell, *The Women's Army Corps*, pp. 318-320, 369-370

12. Ibid., pp. 383-384

13. Mary C. Lyne and Kay Arthur, Lieutenants, USCR(W), *Three Years Behind the Mast: The Story of the United States Coast Guard SPARS* (Washington, D.C., n.p., 1946), pp. 90-93

14. *The Women's Army Corps*, CMH Pub 72-15 (Washington, D.C.: U. S. Center for Military History, n.d.), pp. 21-22.

15. *The New York Times Magazine*, 3 December 1944, pp. 18-19; Judith A. Bellafaire, *The Army Nurse Corps*, CMH Pub 72-14 (Washington, D.C.: U. S. Center of Military History, n.d.), p. 16

16. Morden, *The Women's Army Corps*, p. 19; United States of America, 50th Anniversary of World War II Commemoration Committee, Fact Sheets: *Women in the Navy, Women Marines in WWII*; Lyne, *Three Years Behind the Mast*, pp. 108-110

17. *The New York Times*, 16 August 1943, p.16; Doris Weatherford, *American Women and World War II* (New York: Facts on File, 1990), p. 21; Deborah G. Douglas, *United States Women in Aviation, 1940-1985* (Washington, D.C.: Smithsonian Institution Press, 1991), p. 17; Treadwell, *The Women's Army Corps*, p. 393; *The New York Times*, 25 May 1944, p. 23; *The New York Times*, 3 September 1943, p. 16

NOTES TO CHAPTER 10
Women in Aviation

1. Charles P. May, *Women in Aeronautics* (New York: Thomas Nelson & Sons, 1962), pp. 66-96, 154; Deborah G. Douglas, *United States Women in Aviation, 1940-1985* (Washington, D.C.: Smithsonian Institution Press, 1991), p. 4; David Roberts, "Men Didn't Have to Prove They Could Fly, but Women Did," *Smithsonian*, August 1944, pp. 72-74, 78; Doris L. Rich, *Queen Bess: Daredevil Aviator* (Washington, D.C.: Smithsonian Institution Press, 1993) pp. 31-35, 49, 51, 53-62, 72-73, 110

2. Douglas, *United States Women in Aviation*, pp. 27-56, 100-101; Lettice Curtis, *The Forgotten Pilots: A Story of the Air Transport Auxiliary, 1939-45* (Henly-on-Thames: G.T. Foulis & Co., 1971), pp. 141-146

3. Bettie J. Morden, *The Women's Army Corps*, 1945-1978 (Washington D.C.: U.S. Army Center of Military History, 1990), p. 20; *The Women's Army Corps*, CMH Pub 72-15 (Washington, D.C.: U. S. Army Center of Military History, n.d.), pp. 11-12

4. Douglas, *United States Women in Aviation*, pp. 36-40; U.S. Department of the Navy, "3rd Year, WAVES Number 86,000," *All Hands*, Bureau of Naval Personnel Information Bulletin, August, 1945, p. 16; Jean Ebbert and Marie-Beth Hall, *Crossed Currents: Navy Women from WWI to Tailhook* (Washington, D.C.: Brassey's (U.S.), 1993), p. 70; Peter A. Soderbergh, *Women Marines: The World War II Era* (Westport, Conn.: Praeger Publishers, 1992), p. 91; Lt. Elizabeth Tudor Scullin, USMCWR, "Out-Marining the Marines," *Marine Corps Gazette*, April 1944, p. 47; U.S. Coast Guard Auxiliary, 13th Naval District, *Norwester*, Annual Edition, 1945 (Seattle, Wash.: U.S. Coast Guard Auxiliary, 1945), p. 117

5. May, *Women in Aeronautics*, pp. 162-170; *The New York Times*, 7 December 1942, p. 20; Darlene Clark Hine, ed., *Black Women in America: An Historical Encyclopedia*, vol. 1 (New York: Carlson Publishing, 1993), s.v., Bragg, p. 160-161

NOTES TO CHAPTER 11
Dawn of the Electronic Age

1. Jean Ebbert and Marie-Beth Hall, *Crossed Currents: Navy Women from WWI to Tailhook* (Washington, D.C.: Brassey's (U.S.), 1993), p. 75, 53-54; United States of America, 50th Anniversary of World War II Commemoration Committee, Fact Sheet: *Women in the Navy* (Washington, D.C.: n.p., 1994); U.S. Coast Guard, Public Information Division, *The Coast Guard at War: Women's Reserve*, vol. 22 A (Washington, D.C.: U.S. Coast Guard, (April 15), 1948), p. 209; David Kahn, *The Codebreakers: The Story of Secret Writing* (New York: The Macmillan Company, 1967), p. 417-418; Michael Gannon, *Operation Drumbeat: The Dramatic True Story of Germany's First U-Boat Attack Along the American Coast in World War II* (New York: Harper & Row Publishers, 1990), p. 162; Dr. Kathleen Williams, author, "Huff Duff: The U.S. Navy and the Battle of the Atlantic," forthcoming book from the Naval Institute Press, Interview by phone, 5 July 1995

2. Mary "Ginny" Blakemore Johnston, Interview by telephone, 13 July 1995; Samuel Eliot Morison, *The Two-Ocean War: A Short History of the United States Navy in the Second World War* (Boston: Little, Brown and Company, 1963), pp. 493-511

3. Mary C. Lyne and Kay Arthur, *Three Years Behind the Mast: The Story of the United States Coast Guard SPARS* (Washington, D.C.: n.p., 1946), pp. 115-117

4. *The New York Times*, 3 January 1992, p. A17; Ebbert, *Crossed Currents*, p. 101

NOTES TO CHAPTER 12
Women and Weaponry

1. Mattie E. Treadwell, *The Women's Army Corps*, United States Army in World War II, Special Studies (Washington, D.C.: Department of the Army, Office of the Chief of Military History, 1954), pp. 552-553; Bettie J. Morden, *The Women's Army Corps, 1945-1978* (Washington, D.C.: U.S. Army Center of Military History, 1990), p. 14; Joy Bright Hancock, *Lady in the Navy: A Personal Reminiscence* (Annapolis, Md.:The Naval Institute Press, 1972) pp. 140-142

.2. Pat Meid, *Marine Corps Women's Reserve in World War II* (Washington, D.C.: Headquarters, U.S. Marine Corps, February 1964) p. 16

3. Stremlow, *Free a Marine to Fight*, p. 10; Jean Horsfall, Telephone interview, 25 November 1994; Robin J. Thomson, PA2, USCG, *The Coast Guard & the Women's Reserve in World War II* (Washington, D.C.: U.S. Coast Guard, 1992), p. 6; Betty Splaine, CWO, USCG (Ret.), Telephone interview, December 1994; U.S. Department of the Navy, Library, Telephone interview, 12 December 1994

4. C. Kay Larson, "The Coast Guard Auxiliary in World War II (Paper prepared for U.S. Coast Guard Auxiliary, First Coast Guard District, Southern Region, World War II Commemoration Committee, 1994), pp. 8-9

5. Treadwell, *The Women's Army Corps*, pp. 301-302; Bettie J. Morden, *The Women's Army Corps, 1945-1978* (Washington, D.C.: U.S. Army Center of Military History, 1990), pp. 20-21; *Defense of the Americas* (Washington, D.C.: U.S. Government Printing Office, 1991), p. 18

NOTES TO CHAPTER 13
Over There

1. Edward D. Rosenbaum, "Wartime Nurses," *New Choices for the Best Years*, July 1989, pp. 24-28; Judith A. Bellafaire, *The Army Nurse Corps*, CMH Pub 72-14 (Washington, D.C.: Center of Military History, n.d.), pp. 9-10; Doris Weatherford, *American Women and World War II* (New York: Facts on File, 1990), p. 9

2. Alma Lutz, ed., *With Love, Jane: Letters from American Women on the War Fronts* (New York: John Day Company, 1945), p. 80; Bettie J. Morden, *The Women's Army Corps, 1945-1978* (Washington, D.C.: U. S. Army Center of Military History, 1992), p. 22; Vida M. Ganoni, *The 149th WAAC Post HQ CO: Our Story, 1942/1943* (privately published, 1993) pp. 5-7, 21-34

3. Charles R. Anderson, *The U.S. Army Campaigns of World War II: Tunisia, November 17, 1942-May 13, 1943*, CMH Pub 72-12 (Washington, D.C.: Center of Military History, n.d.), pp. 5-17; Doris Weatherford, *American Women and World War II* (New York: Facts on File, 1990), p. 9

4. Bellafaire, *The Army Nurse Corps*, pp. 11-13; *New York Times Magazine*, 3 December 1944, pp. 18-19

5. Bellafaire, *The Army Nurse Corps*, pp. 11-15; *New York Times Magazine*, 15 August 1943, pp. 18-19

6. Judy Bennett Litoff and David C. Smith, *We're in This War, Too: World War II Letters from American Women in Uniform* (New York: Oxford University Press, 1994), p. 130

7. Jean-Claude Baker and Chris Chase, *Josephine: The Hungry Heart* (New York: Random House, 1993), pp. 226-263, 365-366

NOTES TO CHAPTER 14
The European Mainland

1. Bettie J. Morden, *The Women's Army Corps, 1945-1978* (Washington, D.C.: U. S. Army Center of Military History, 1990), p. 22; Judith A. Bellafaire, *The Women's Army Corps*, CMH Pub 72-15 (Washington, D.C.: Center of Military History, n.d.), p. 19.

2. Andrew J. Birtle, *The U.S. Army Campaigns of World War II: Sicily, 9 July - 17 August 1943* CMH Pub 72-16 (Washington, D.C.: Center of Military History, 1993) p. 3

3..Bellafaire, *The Women's Army Corps*, p. 16-17

4. Doris Weatherford, *American Women and World War II* (New York: Facts on File, 1990), p.10; Judith A. Bellafaire, *The Army Nurse Corps*, CMH Pub 72-14 (Washington, D.C.: Center of Military History, n.d.), pp. 16-17

5. Morden, *The Women's Army Corps*, p. 22; The Women's Army Corps, p. 15; Mattie E. Treadwell, *The Women's Army Corps, United States Army in World War II, Special Studies* (Washington, D.C.: Department of the Army, Office of the Chief of Military History, 1954), p. 367; Bellafaire, *The Army Nurse Corps*, p. 15

6. Bellafaire, *The Army Nurse Corps*, pp. 17-18.

7. *Ibid.*, pp. 18-20.

6. *The New York Times*, 24 May 1944, p. 10.

9. Listing of Army Nurse Corps Memorials, Photocopied (Washington, D.C.: Center of Military History, n.d..); Bellafaire, *The Women's Army Corps: A Commemoration of World War II Service* CMH Pub 72-15 (Washington, D.C.: Center of Military History, n.d.) p. 13; Robert V. Piemonte and Cindy Gurney eds., *Highlights in the History of the Army Nurse Corps* (Washington, D.C.: Center of Military History, 1987), p. 93.

NOTES TO CHAPTER 15
Pacific and Far East

1. Mattie E. Treadwell, *United States Army in World War II: Special Studies: The Women's Army Corps* (Washington, D.C.: Department of the Army, 1954) pp. 420-422, 426

2. Judith A. Bellafaire, *The Women's Army Corps* CMH Pub 72-15 (Washington, D.C.: Center of Military History, n.d.) p. 23

3. Mattie E. Treadwell, *The Women's Army Corps*, United States Army in World War II, Special Studies (Washington, D.C.: Department of the Army, Office of the Chief of Military History, 1954), pp. 420-50; Bellafaire, *The Women's Army Corps*, p. 24; Bettie J. Morden, *The Women's Army Corps, 1945-1978* (Washington, D.C.: U. S. Army Center of Military History, 1990), p. 23; Doris Weatherford, *American Women and World War II* (New York: Facts on File, 1990), p. 87

4. Treadwell, *The Women's Army Corps*, pp. 464-467, 471, 473

5. Michael Stevens, ed., *Voices of the Wisconsin Past: Women Remember the War, 1941-1945* (Madison, Wis.: State Historical Society of Wisconsin, 1993), p. 67-69; *The New York Times*, 4 January 1943, p. 12;

The Women's Army Corps, p. 24; Barbara Tomlin, "Beyond Paradise: The U.S. Navy Nurse Corps in the Pacific in World War II" (Part One), *MINERVA: Quarterly Report on Women and the Military* vol. 11, no. 2 (Summer 1993), p. 42; Barbara Tomlin, "Beyond Paradise: The U.S. Navy Nurse Corps in the Pacific in World War II" (Part Two), *MINERVA: Quarterly Report on Women and the Military* vol. 11, no. 3/4 (Fall/Winter 1993), p. 52; Robert V. Piemonte and Cindy Gurney, eds., *Highlights in the History of the Army Nurse Corps* (Washington, D.C.: Center of Military History, 1987), p. 17

4. Maxine Lerch, R.N., "Merchant Marine Nursing," *American Journal of Nursing*, vol. 44, no. 3 (September 1944), pp. 846-847; Mary C. Lyne and Kay Arthur, *Three Years Behind the Mast: The Story of the United States Coast Guard SPARS* (Washington, D.C.: n.p., 1944), p. 93-97

NOTES TO CHAPTER 16
The D-Day Invasion

1. Dwight D. Eisenhower, *Crusade into Europe*, (New York: Doubleday, 1948) pp. 226-231

2. Judith A. Bellafaire, *The Women's Army Corps*, CMH Pub 72-15 (Washington, D.C.: Center of Military History, n.d.), pp. 19-21

3. Alma Lutz, *With Love, Jane: Letters from American Women on the War Fronts* (New York: John Day Company, 1945) p. 90

4. Lutz, *With Love, Jane* pp. 108-109; Judith A. Bellafaire,*Women's Army Corps* CMH Pub 72-15 (Washington, D.C.: Center of Military History, n.d.) p. 21

5. Bellafaire, *The Army Nurse Corps*, p. 20; *The New York Times*, 18 June 1944, p. 6; *The New York Times Magazine*, 3 December 1944, pp. 18-19

6. Lutz, *With Love, Jane*, pp. 24, 30

7. Ibid., p. 14

8. Ibid., pp. 115, 119; Bellafaire, *The Women's Army Corps*, p. 21

9. Lutz, *With Love, Jane*, pp. 9-10

10. Ibid., pp. 30-32, 36

11. *The New York Times Magazine*, 24 October 1943, p. 18

12. Mattie E. Treadwell, *United States Army in World War II: Special Studies: The Women's Army Corps* (Washington, D.C.: Department of the Army, 1954) p. 388

13. Lutz, *With Love, Jane*, p. 57-58; *The U.S. Army Campaigns of World War II: A Brief History of the U.S. Army in World War II* (Washington, D.C.: Center of Military History, 1992), p. 20; Women's Army Corps Museum, *A Date With Destiny* (Ft. McClellan, Ala.: Women's Army Corps Foundation, 1984), p. 7

14. Robert V. Piemonte and Cindy Gurney, eds., *Highlights in the History of the Army Nurse Corps* (Washington, D.C.: Center of Military History, 1987), p. 17; Bellafaire, *The Army Nurse Corps*, p. 22

15. Listing of Army Nurse Corps Memorials. Photocopied (Washington, D.C.: Center of Military History, n.d.)

16. Eisenhower, *Crusade in Europe*, pp. 258-260

17. David Eisenhower, *Eisenhower: At War, 1943-1945* (London: William Collins Sons & Co., 1986), pp. 348-49, 329, 299-300

18. Bellafaire, *The Women's Army Corps*, p. 21, 25; Eisenhower, *Eisenhower at War*, p. 348

19. Lutz, *With Love, Jane*, p. 122

20. Lutz, *With Love, Jane*, p. 122; U.S. Department of the Navy, "The Task Force in White," *All Hands*, Naval Personnel Information Bulletin, March 1945, p. 25

21. Orth to Yorke, March 1945. Hazel Yorke Valley private papers in possession of J. A. V. Harlan

22. Bellafaire, *The Army Nurse Corps*, p. 23; *The New York Times*, 29 March 1945, p.2

23. Bellafaire, *The Women's Army Corps*, p. 22; Bellafaire, *The Army Nurse Corps*, p. 20

NOTE TO CHAPTER 17
American Women in the French Resistance

1. Margaret Rossiter, *Women in the Resistance*, (New York: Praeger Publishers, 1986), pp. 16-17, 119, 189-216

NOTES TO CHAPTER 18
The Final Months in the Pacific

1. Judith A. Bellafaire, *The Army Nurse Corps* CMH Pub 72-14 (Washington, D.C.: Center of Military History, n.d.) p. 27

2. Barbara Tomlin, "Beyond Paradise: The U.S. Navy Nurse Corps in the Pacific in World War II (Part Two)." *MINERVA: Quarterly Report on Women and the Military,* vol. XI, no. 3/4 (Fall/Winter 1993) p. 43; *The New York Times,* 3 April 1945, pp. 1, 4

3. Ibid, pp. 46-47

4. Peter A. Soderberg, *Women Marines: The World War II Era* (Westport, CT: Praeger Publishers, 1992) pp. 84-85

5. Bellafaire, *The Army Nurse Corps,* p. 29

6. *The New York Times,* 12 March 1945, p. 10; USA 50th COMC, *Fact Sheet: Women in the Navy*

7. *The New York Times,* 20 August 1944, p. 10

8. Shelley Mydans, "Flight Nurse," *Life,* February 12, 1945

9. *The New York Times,* 9 June 1945, p. 1; *The New York Times* 10 July 1945, p.2; John Masters, *The Road Past Mandalay* (London: Michael Joseph, Ltd., 1961) pp. 185-86

10. Bellafaire, *The Army Nurse Corps,* p. 28

11. Treadwell, *The Women's Army Corps,* pp. 428-435.

12. Robert Ross Smith, *Triumph in the Philippines* (Washington, D.C.: Department of the Army, 1984), pp. 251-56; R. Renton Hind, *Spirits Unbroken,* (n.p., 1946) p. 279

13. *The New York Times,* 28 July 1945, p.13; USCG, *All Hands,* October 1945, p. 4; *The New York Times,* 8 November 1947, p.20; *The Ithaca Journal,* March 6, 1995, p.1

14. *.The New York Times,* 26 February, 1945, p. 21

15. Barbara Tomlin, "Beyond Paradise: The U.S. Navy Corps in the Pacific in World War II (Part One)." *MINERVA: Quarterly Report on Women and the Military,* vol. XI, no. 2 (Summer 1993) p. 39

16. *The New York Times,* 7 February 1945, p.4; *The New York Times,* 27 February 1945, p. 13

NOTES TO CHAPTER 19
Civilian Organizations

1. Michael Stevens, ed., *Voices of the Wisconsin Past: Women Remember the War, 1941-1945* (Madison, Wis.: State Historical Society of Wisconsin, 1993) pp. 96-97

2. Ibid., p. 76

3. *The New York Times*, April 12, 1945, p.8

4. *The New York Times*, March 12, 1948, p.25

5. *The New York Times*, August 20, 1944, p.10

6. USA50thCOMC, Fact Sheet: *USO in World War II*

7. *The New York Times*, October 20, 1994, p. B16

8. *The New York Times*, January 22, 1942, p. 14

9. C.M. Schulten, *Zeg Mij Aan Wien Ik Tebehoor* (Amsterdam: Rijksinstituut Voor Oorlogsdocumentatie, 1990) pp. 94-95

10. Thomas J. Cutler, *Brown Water, Black Berets: Coastal and Riverine Warfare in Vietnam* (Annapolis: MD, Naval Institute Press, 1988) p. 67; Lina Mainero, *American Women Writers* (New York: Frederick K. Unger Publishing Co., Inc., 1979) pp. 331-33

11. Frederick S. Voss, *Reporting the War*, pp. 81-93

NOTES TO CHAPTER 20
At Work on the Homefront

1. Michael Stevens, ed., *Voices of the Wisconsin Past: Women Remember the War, 1941-1945* (Madison, WI: State Historical Society of Wisconsin, 1993) p. 9

2. South Street Seaport Museum & The Seaman's Church Institute. "Remembering the Port of New York During World War II," Conference Brochure (New York, 1993)

3. Stevens, *Voices of the Wisconsin Past*, pp. 9-15

4. USA50th COMC, Fact Sheet: *Liberty Ships in World War II*; Richard Hall, *Patriots in Disguise*, (New York: Paragon House, 1993), pp. 164-166

5. USA50th COMC, *Fact Sheets: Native Americans, Hispanic-Americans*

6. C. Kay Larson,, "The Coast Guard Auxiliary in World War II," Paper prepared for U.S. Coast Guard Auxiliary, First Coast Guard District, Southern Region, World War II Commemoration Committee, 1994, p.5;

Mary C. Lyne and Kay Arthur, *Three Years Behind the Mast: The Story of the United States Coast Guard SPARS* (n.p.) p. 119; *The New York Times*, 30 January 1943, p. 12

7. Lyne and Arthur, *Three Years Behind the Mast*, pp. 117-18

NOTES TO CHAPTER 21
Allied Women

1. *The New York Times*, 4 February 1943, p. 26

2. Margaret Rossiter, *Women in the Resistance* (New York: Praeger Publishers, 1986), pp. 23-45, 127-29

3. Leonoor Waganaar and Patricia Steur, *De Laaste Ridders* (The Hague: SDU Uitgeveri, 1990), pp. 111-20; Dr. C. M. Schulten, *Zeg Mij Aan Wien Ik Toebehoor* (Amsterdam: Rijksinstitut Voor Oorlogsdocumentatie, 1990), *passim*; William Stevenson, *A Man Called Intrepid* (New York: Random House, Ballantine Books, 1982), pp. 57, 62-63

4. *The New York Times*, 4 February 1943, p. 26

5. *New York Newsday*, 6 October 1994, pp. B4-5

6. Morris Rosenblum, *Heroes of Israel* (New York: Fleet Press Corporation, 1972), pp. 72-75

7. Lettice Curtis, *The Forgotten Pilots: A Story of the Air Transport Auxiliary, 1939-45* (Henley-on-Thames: G. T. Foulis & Co., 1971), pp. 144, 153; *The New York Times*, 28 April 1947, p. 28

8. *The New York Times*, 5 February 1942, p. 18

9. U.S.S.R. Ministry of Defense, *The Soviet Air Force in World War II*, trans. Leland Fetzer, ed. Ray Wagner (Garden City, N.J.: Doubleday & Company, 1973), p. 156; Cheryl MeElroy, SSgt., USA, "Women at War? World History is Full of Examples," *Army Times*, 8 August 1994, p. 34

10. Richard Hough, *Edwina: Countess Mountbatten of Burma* (New York: William Morrow and Company, 1984), pp. 148-152

11. Winston S. Churchill, *The Second World War: Closing the Ring* (Boston: Houghton Mifflin Company, 1951), pp. 66-68; Marjorie Fletcher, *The WRNS: A History of the Women's Royal Naval Service* (Annapolis, Md.: Naval Institute Press, 1989), pp. 73-78

12. Stevenson, *Intrepid*, pp. 235-253; Rossiter, *Women in the Resistance*, pp. 168-81

NOTES TO CHAPTER 22
Conclusion

1. Mary C. Stremlow, *Free a Marine to Fight: Women Marines in World War II* (Washington, D.C.: Marine Corps Headquarters, History and Museums Division, 1994), pp. 35-36

2. Franklin D. Roosevelt, "State of the Union Speech," *U.S. Congressional Record*, January 1945, part 1, p. 93; Doris Weatherford, *American Women and World War II* (New York: Facts on File, 1990), p. 19

3. Robert V. Piemonte and Cindy Gurney, eds., *Highlights in the History of the Army Nurse Corps* (Washington, D.C.: Center of Military History, 1987), p. 18; Judith A. Bellafaire, *The Women's Army Corps*, CMH Pub 72-14 (Washington, D.C.: Center of Military History, n.d.), pp. 24-25; United States of America, 50th Anniversary of World War II Commemoration Committee, *Fact Sheet: Women in the Navy* (Washington, D.C.: n.p., 1994); Mary C. Lyne and Kay Arthur, *Three Years Behind the Mast: The Story of the United States Coast Guard SPARs* (Washington, D.C.: n.p., 1946), pp. 111-112

4. Piemonte, *Highlights in the History of the Army Nurse Corps*, pp. 91-92; "Listing of Army Nurse Corps Memorials," Photocopied (Washington, D.C.: Center of Military History, Office of the Army Nurse Corps Historian, n.d.)

5. Commemoration Committee, Fact Sheet: *Women Marines in World War II*; Peter A. Soderbergh, *Women Marines: The World War II Era* (Westport, Conn.: Praeger Publishers, 1992), pp. xv-xvi

6. Betty Splaine, ed., *SPARs, 50th Anniversary Edition*, SPAR Notes No. 8 (n.p.), p. 11

7. Samuel Eliot Morison, *History of United States Naval Operations in World War II: The Battle of the Atlantic, September 1939 - May 1943*, vol. I (Boston: Little, Brown and Company, 1988), p. 171; U.S. Department of the Navy, *All Hands*, Bureau of Naval Personnel Information Bulletin, August 1944, p. 41; U.S. Coast Guard, Historian's Office, Washington, D.C., Telephone interview, 11 September 1995

8. Bettie J. Morden, *The Women's Army Corps, 1945-1978* (Washington, D.C.: U.S. Army, Center of Military History, 1990), p. 26; *The New York Times*, 24 April 1944, p. 10

9. Piemonte, *Highlights in the History of the Army Nurse Corps*, p. 19

List of Sources Cited

Books and Periodicals

Anderson, Charles R. *The U.S. Army Campaigns of World War II: Tunisia, 17 November 1942 - 13 May 1943*. CMH Pub 72-12. Washington, D.C.: Center of Military History, n.d.

Bailey, Jennifer L. *The U.S. Army Campaigns of World War II: Philippine Islands, 7 December 1941 - 10 May 1943*. CMH Pub 72-3. Washington, D.C.: Center of Military History, 1992.

Baker, Jean-Claude and Chris Chase. *Josephine: The Hungry Heart*. New York: Random House, 1993.

Bellafaire, Judith A. *The Army Nurse Corps*. CMH Pub 72-14. Washington, D.C.: Center of Military History, n.d.

_____. *The Women's Army Corps: CMH Pub 72-15*. Washington, D.C.: Center of Military History, n.d.

Birtle, Andrew J. *The U.S. Army Campaigns of World War II: Sicily, 9 July - 17 August 1943*. CMH Pub 72-16. Washington, D.C.: Center of Military History, 1993.

Bishop, Eleanor C. *Prints in the Sand: The U.S. Coast Guard During World War II*. Missoula, Mont.: Pictorial Histories Publishing Co., 1989.

Bombard, Charles F., Wynona Bice-Stephens, and Karen L.Ferguson.. "The Soldiers' Nurse: Colonel Florence A. Blanchfield." *MINERVA: Quarterly Report on Women and the Military* (Winter 1988), pp. 43-49.

Churchill, Winston S. *The Second World War: Closing the Ring.* Boston: Houghton Mifflin Company, 1951.

_____. *The Second World War: The Hinge of Fate.* Boston: Houghton Mifflin Company, 1950.

Condon-Rall, Mary Ellen. "U.S. Army Medical Preparations and the Outbreak of War: The Philippines, 1941 - 6 May 1942." *The Journal of Military History* (January 1992), pp. 35-36.

Costello, John. *The Pacific War, 1941-1945.* New York: William Morrow and Company, 1981.

Curtis, Lettice. *The Forgotten Pilots: A Story of the Air Transport Auxiliary, 1939-45.* Henley-on-Thames: G. T. Foulis & Co., 1971.

Cutler, Thomas J. *Brown Water, Black Berets: Coastal and Riverine Warfare in Vietnam.* Annapolis, Md.: Naval Institute Press, 1988.

Douglas, Deborah G. *United States Women in Aviation, 1940-1985.* Washington, D.C.: Smithsonian Institution Press, 1991.

Ebbert, Jean, and Marie-Beth Hall. *Crossed Currents: Navy Women from WWI to Tailhook.* Washington, D.C.: Brassey's (U.S.), 1993.

Eisenhower, David. *Eisenhower: At War, 1943-1945.* London: William Collins Sons & Co., 1986.

Eisenhower, Dwight D. *Crusade in Europe.* New York: Doubleday, 1948.

Fletcher, M[arjorie]. H. *The WRNS: A History of the Women's Royal Naval Service.* Annapolis, Md.: Naval Institute Press, 1989.

Francillon, Rene. *Grumman Aircraft Since 1929.* Annapolis, Md.: Naval Institute Press, 1989.

Frank, Mary E. V. "Army and Navy Nurses Held as Prisoners of War During World War II," *MINERVA: Quarterly Report on Women and the Military* (Summer 1988), pp. 82-90.

Gannon, Michael. *Operation Drumbeat: The Dramatic True Story of Germany's First U-Boat Attack Along the American Coast in World War II.* New York: Harper & Row Publishers, 1990.

Ganoni, Vida M. *The 149th WAAC Post HQ CO: Our Story, 1942/1943.* Privately published, 1993.

Goodell, Jane. *They Sent Me to Iceland.* New York: Ives Washburn, 1943.

Hall, Richard. *Patriots in Disguise: Women Warriors of the Civil War.* New York: Paragon House, 1993.

Hancock, Joy Bright. *Lady in the Navy: A Personal Reminiscence.* Annapolis, Md.: The Naval Institute Press, 1972.

Hickam, Homer, Jr. *Torpedo Junction: U-Boat War Off America's East Coast, 1942.* Annapolis, Md.: Naval Institute Press, 1989.

Hind, R. Renton. *Spirits Unbroken* .n.p.., 1946.

Hine, Darlene Clark, ed. *Black Women in America: An Historical Encyclopedia.* Vol. 1. New York: Carlson Publishing, 1993.

Holm, Jeanne.. *Women in the Military: An Unfinished Revolution.* Novato, Cal.: Presidio Press, 1982.

Hough, Richard. *Edwina: Countess Mountbatten of Burma.* New York: William Morrow and Company, 1984.

Hunter, J. H. *Adrift: The Story of Twenty Days on a Raft in the South Atlantic.* Grand Rapids, Mich.: Zonedevan Publishing House, 1943.

Johnson, Robert Erwin. *Coast Guard Manned Naval Vessels in World War II.* Washington, D.C.: U.S. Coast Guard, 1993.

Kahn, David, *The Codebreakers: The Story of Secret Writing.* New York: The Macmillan Company, 1967.

Larson, C. Kay. "The Coast Guard Auxiliary in World War II." Paper prepared for U.S. Coast Guard Auxiliary, First Coast Guard District, Southern Region, World War II Commemoration Committee, 1994.

Lerch, Maxine. "Merchant Marine Nursing." *American Journal of Nursing* (September 1944): 846-47.

Litoff, Judy Bennett and David C. Smith. *We're in This War, Too: World War II Letters from American Women in Uniform.* New York: Oxford University Press, 1994.

Lutz, Alma, ed. *With Love, Jane: Letters from American Women on the War Fronts.* New York: John Day Company, 1945.

Lyne, Mary C., and Kay Arthur. *Three Years Behind the Mast: The Story of the United States Coast Guard SPARS.* Washington, D.C.: n.p., 1946.

Mainero, Lina, ed. *American Women Writers.* New York: Frederick K. Unger Publishing Co., 1979.

Manchester, William. *America's Caesar: Douglas MacArthur, 1880-1964.* Boston: Little, Brown and Company, 1988.

_____. *The Last Lion: Winston Spencer Churchill, Alone 1932-1940*. Boston: Little, Brown and Company, 1988.

Masters, John. *The Road Past Mandalay*. London: Michael Joseph, 1961.

May, Charles P. *Women in Aeronautics*. New York: Thomas Nelson & Sons, 1962.

McElroy, Cheryl. "Women at War? World History is Full of Examples." *Army Times*, 8 August 1994, p. 35.

McIntosh, Elizabeth T. *The Role of Women in Intelligence*. McLean, VA: Association of Former Intelligence Officers, 1989.

Meid, Pat. *Marine Corps Women's Reserve in World War II*. Washington, D.C.: Headquarters, U.S. Marine Corps, February 1964.

Morden, Bettie J. *The Women's Army Corps, 1945-1978*. Washington, D. C.: U.S. Army Center of Military History, 1990.

Morison, Samuel Eliot. *History of United States Naval Operations in World War II: The Battle of the Atlantic, September 1939 - May 1943*. Vol. 1. Boston: Little, Brown and Company, 1947.

_____. *History of United States Naval Operations in World War II; The Invasion of France and Germany, 1944-1945*. Vol. 11. Boston: Little, Brown and Company, 1957.

_____. *The Two-Ocean War: A Short History of the United States Navy in the Second World War*. Boston: Little, Brown and Company, 1963.

Morton, Louis. *The War in the Pacific: The Fall of the Philippines, United States Army in World War II.* Washington, D.C.: Department of the Army, Office of the Chief of Military History, 1953.

Mydans, Shelley. "Flight Nurse." *Life,* 12 February 1945

Orth to Yorke. March 1945. Hazel Yorke Valley private papers in possession of J. A. V. Harlan.

"Permanent WAVES." *Newsweek,* 10 August 1942, pp. 30-32.

Piemonte, Robert V.and Cindy Gurney, eds. *Highlights in the History of the Army Nurse Corps.*CMH Pub 85-1. Washington, D.C.: Center of Military History, 1987.

Potter, E. B. *Nimitz.* Annapolis, Md.: Naval Institute Press, 1976.

Rich, Doris L. *Queen Bess: Daredevil Aviator.* Washington, D.C.: Smithsonian Institution Press, 1993.

Roberts, David. "Men Didn't Have to Prove They Could Fly, but Women Did." *Smithsonian,* August 1994, pp. 72-81.

Roosevelt, Franklin D. "State of the Union Message." *Congressional Record: House,* 79th Cong., 1st Sess., vol. 91, pt. 1, p. 93.

Rosenbaum, Edward D. "Wartime Nurses." *New Choices for the Best Years,* July 1989, pp. 24-28.

Rosenblum, Morris. *Heroes of Israel.* New York: Fleet Press Corporation, 1972.

Rossiter, Margaret. *Women in the Resistance.* New York: Praeger Publishers, 1986.

Schulten, C.M. *Zeg Mij Aan Wien Ik Toebehoor*. Amsterdam: Rijksinstituut VoorOorlogsdocumentatie, 1990.

Scullin, Elizabeth Tudor.. "Out-Marining the Marines." *Marine Corps Gazette*, April 1944, pp. 45-49.

Sicherman, Barbara, and Carol Hurd Green, eds. *Notable American Women, The Modern Period: A Biographical Dictionary*. Cambridge, Mass.: The Belknap Press of Harvard University Press, 1980.

Singh, Sukhwindar. "General Vaught Talks About American Women Veterans." *Social Education*, vol. 58 (February 1994), pp. 98-100.

Smith, Robert Ross. *United States Army in World War II: The War in the Pacific: Triumph in the Philippines*. United States Armyin World War II. Washington, D.C.: Center of Military History, 1963.

Soderbergh, Peter A. *Women Marines: The World War II Era*. Westport, Conn.: Praeger Publishers, 1992.

South Street Seaport Museum & The Seaman's Church Institute. *Remembering the Port of New York During World War II*. Conference Brochure, New York, NY, 1993.

Spangler, Keith, PAI, USCG. "Airborne at 77." *Commandant's Bulletin*, January 1977, pp. 12-16.

Splaine, Betty, ed. *SPARS, 50th Anniversary Edition*. SPAR Notes No. 8. Washington, D.C.: n.p., 1992.

Stevens, Michael, ed. *Voices of the Wisconsin Past: Women Remember the War, 1941-1945*. Madison, Wis.: State Historical Society of Wisconsin, 1993.

Stevenson, William. *A Man Called Intrepid*. New York: Random House, Ballantine Books, 1982.

Stremlow, Mary C. *Free a Marine to Fight: Women Marines in World War II*. Washington, D. C.: Marine Corps Headquarters, History and Museums Division, 1994.

Thomson, Robin J. *The Coast Guard & the Women's Reserve in World War II*. Washington, D.C.: U.S. Coast Guard, 1992.

Thruelsen, Richard. *The Grumman Story*. New York: Praeger Publishers,1978.

Tomlin, Barbara. "Beyond Paradise: The U.S. Navy Nurse Corps in the Pacific in World War II (Part One)." *MINERVA: Quarterly Report on Women and the Military* (Summer 1993), pp. 33-53.

_____. "Beyond Paradise: The U.S. Navy Nurse Corps in the Pacific in World War II (Part Two)." *MINERVA: Quarterly Report on Women and the Military* (Fall/Winter 1993), pp. 37-56.

Treadwell, Mattie E. *United States Army in World War II: Special Studies: The Women's Army Corps*. Washington, D.C.: Department of the Army, 1954.

U.S. Coast Guard. *Coast Guard Magazine*, November 1945, p. 70.

U.S. Coast Guard, Public Information Division. *The Coast Guard at War: The Temporary Component of the Coast Guard Reserve*. Vol. 20. Washington, D.C.: U.S. Coast Guard, January 1, 1948.

_____. *The Coast Guard at War: Women's Reserve*. Vol. 22A. Washington, D.C.: U.S. Coast Guard, April 15, 1948.

U.S. Coast Guard, Third Naval District. *All Hands*, December 1943, p. 6.

_____, Third Naval District. *All Hands*, October 1945, p. 4.

U.S. Coast Guard Auxiliary. "With the U.S. Coast Guard Auxiliary." *Yachting*, March 1943, p. 57.

U.S. Coast Guard Auxiliary, 13th Naval District. *Norwester, Annual Edition, 1945.* Seattle, Wash.: U.S. Coast Guard Auxiliary, 1945.

U.S. Department of the Army. Listing of Army Nurse Corps Memorials. Washington, D.C.: Center of Military History, n.d.

U.S. Department of the Army. Listing of Army Nurse Prisoners-of-War. Washington, D.C.: Center of Military History, n.d.

U.S. Department of the Army. *The U.S Army Campaigns of World War II: A Brief History of the U.S. Army in World War II.* Washington, D.C.: Center of Military History, n.d.

U.S. Department of the Army. *The U.S Army Campaigns of World War II: Defense of the Americas.* Washington, D.C.: Center of Military History, n.d.

U.S. Department of the Navy. *All Hands.* Naval Bureau of Personnel Information Bulletin, August 1944, p. 41.

U.S. Department of the Navy. "Charting the Road to Tokyo." All Hands, Naval Personnel Information Bulletin, October 1944, pp. 24-27.

U.S. Department of the Navy. "Task Force in White." *All Hands*, Naval Personnel Information Bulletin, March 1945, pp. 23-25.

U.S. Department of the Navy. *The Story of You in Navy Blue.* Washington, D.C.: Department of the Navy, 1944.

U.S. Department of the Navy. "3d Year WAVES Number 86,000." *All Hands,* Naval Personnel Information Bulletin, August 1945, pp. 16-17.

United States of America, 50th Anniversary of World War II Commemoration Committee, Fact Sheets: *American Red Cross, African-Americans in World War II, Asian Americans, Hispanic Americans, Liberty Ships in World War II, Native Americans, The Home Front, Tuskegee Airmen, USO in World War II, Women in the Navy, Women in World War II, Women Marines in World War II, World War II.* Washington, D.C.: n.p., 1994.

Voss, Frederick S. *Reporting the War: The Journalistic Coverage of World War II.* Washington, D.C.: Smithsonian Institution Press, 1994.

Waganaar, Leonoor, and PatriciaSteur. *De Laatste Ridders.* The Hague: SDU Uitgeverij,1990.

Wagner, Roy, ed. *The Soviet Air Force in World War II.* Translated by Leland Fetzer. Garden City, N.Y.: Doubleday & Company, Inc., 1973.

Weatherford, Doris. *American Women and World War II.* New York: Facts on File, 1990.

Wilson, W. W. "Modern Conveniences Boon to Only Woman Lighthouse Keeper." *Coast Guard Magazine,* August 1945, pp. 36-37.

Women's Army Corps Museum. "A Date with Destiny" Ft. McClellan, Ala.: Women's Army Corps Foundation, 1984.

Corporations

Grumman Northrop Corporation, Bethpage, N.Y.
Associated Press, World Wide Photo, New York, N.Y.

Military Services

U.S. Department of the Army, Center of Military History,
    Office of the Army Nurse Corps Historian
U.S. Coast Guard, Historian's Office
U.S. Marine Corps Historical Center
U.S. Department of the Navy, Bureau of Medicine and Surgery
U.S. Department of the Navy, Library.
United States of America, 50th Anniversary of World War II
    Commemoration Committee

Newspapers

The Ithaca (N.Y.) Journal
New York Daily News
New York Newsday
The New York Times

Personal Interviews

Judith A. V. Harlan
Jean Horsfall, former member Women Marines
Mary "Ginny" Blakemore Johnston, former WAC
Ida Pollack, former Brooklyn Navy Yard worker
Betty Splaine, Chief Warrant Officer, USCG (Ret.)
Dr. Kathleen Williams, military historian
Marilyn Willis, former WAVE

Suggestions for Further Reading

This book presents a military history of American women in World War II, i.e., what they did in the war whether in or out of uniform. In my opinion, the three best general works on women in the war are Doris Weatherford's *American Women and World War II*; Alma Lutz', *With Love, Jane: Letters from American Women on the War Fronts*; and Judy Litoff's and David Smith's, *We're in This War, Too*. Weatherford's history covers both military and civilian women. Lutz' book contains letters from military, Red Cross, and USO women serving in Europe and the Pacific. Judy Litoff's and David Smith's book contains a large collection of letters from military and Red Cross women stationed abroad and on the homefront. As a result of a ten-year effort, they have also established an archive of over 30,000 letters written by military and civilian women. This is the largest collection of wartime letters ever developed. These holdings are presently being processed for a microfilm edition to be published by Scholarly Resources, Inc.

Most women stationed overseas were in the Army. The small pamphlet published by the Army's Center of Military History is a very good brief history of the Army Nurse Corps during World War II. A full history of the Corps is currently in progress. Mattie Treadwell's history of the Women's Army Corps is a tremendous work (over 800 pages) and contains unit histories, as well as the history of WAC administration, which includes policy, training, and recruitment issues. It also contains a very thought-provoking chapter on women's military leadership which should be read by current leaders. Some of the issues are still relevant and women's military leadership has not been considered a real topic of study (i.e., not just whether women can develop what men consider leadership traits, but whether women and men respond in the same way to different leadership traits). The Center of Military History has also published a condensed history of the WAC in pamphlet form. In 1992, Dr. Martha Putney published *When the Nation Was in Need: Blacks in the Women's Army Corps During WWII*.

Ebbert's and Hall's *Crossed Currents: Navy Women from WWI to Tailhook* is the only history of women in the Navy currently in print. It has chapters on World War II, although it emphasizes administrative history. The best treatment of the Navy Nurse Corps is Barbara Tomlin's two-part series in *MINERVA: Quarterly Report on Women and the Military*, "Beyond Paradise: The U.S. Navy Nurse Corps in the Pacific in World War II," vol 11, nos. 2 & 3/4 (Summer/Fall/Winter, 1993). The only book-length biography of Grace Hopper was written for a juvenile audience by Charlene Billings.

The two major sources for information on the Women Marines were Peter Soderbergh's book, *Women Marines: The World War II Era*, and Col. Mary Stremlow's *Free a Marine to Fight*, published by Marine Corps Headquarters, History and Museums Division. Soderbergh's book is a social history which contains accounts of 146 Women Marine veterans. Stremlow draws from Soderbergh and other Corps histories.

Coast Guard SPARs Mary Lyne and Kay Arthur have published *Three Years Behind the Mast*, which contains administrative history and personal accounts, as well as very amusing excerpts from a cadet diary (e.g., in commenting on her ill-fitting, newly-issued uniform, she wrote, "I look like something that even the tide wouldn't go out with."). A pamphlet on the SPARs has been written by PA2 Robin Thomson, USCG, and published by the Coast Guard Historian's office. Although difficult to obtain, local District publications written during the war often have SPAR accounts.

My major source for the topic of women in aviation was Deborah Douglas' *United States Women in Aviation, 1940-1985*. This is one of a four-volume series on the history of women in aviation published by the Smithsonian Institution Press. There are a number of books on the Women Air Force Service Pilots. Some titles include: Sally Kiel's *Those Wonderful Women in Their Flying Machines: The Unknown Heroines of World War II*, Ann Noggle's *For God, Country and the Thrill of It: Women Airforce Service Pilots in World War II*, Charles Planck's *Women with Wings*, Adela Scharr's *Sisters in the Sky*, and Winifred Wood's *We Were WASPS: The Story*. Jacqueline Cochran also wrote her autobiography. In 1986, Judith Barger published *Coping with War: An Oral History of United States Army Flight Nurses Who Flew with the Army Air Forces in World War II*. Dr. Patricia Chamings at the University of North Carolina in Greensboro and others are currently researching a history of flight nurses from World War II to the present. Prior to the war, Chicago was a center of black aviation and recently a biography of Bessie Coleman, *Queen Bess*, has been published. An encyclopedia entry on Janet Harmon Bragg indicates that nothing has been published on her. She is still living in Arizona.

Margaret Rossiter's book, *Women in the Resistance*, is a must for a study of the French Resistance. Two very good books on British military women are Marjorie Fletcher's history of the Women's Royal Naval Service and Eric Taylor's *Women Who Went to War, 1938-1946*. They provide broad coverage of duties and war-time experiences. Phyllis Pearsall's book *Women at War* contains delightful contemporary sketches of British women and would be a good school library book. An international juvenile book is Fiona Reynoldson's *World War II: Women in War*, which contains an excellent collection of photographs, although a few are gruesome and graphic. Edwina Mountbatten is one of my heroes and Richard Hough's biography of her is very readable, as is his biography of her husband, Lord Louis, entitled *Mountbatten*. Two books written on the Russian women combat pilots are Bruce Myles' *Night Witches, The Untold Story of Soviet Women in Combat* and Anne Noggle's *A Dance with Death: Soviet Airwomen in World War II*.

During the decade it has been in publication, *MINERVA: Quarterly Report on Women and the Military* has produced numerous articles on women in World War II, including many oral histories. Frederick Voss' newly published, *Reporting the War: The Journalistic Coverage of World War II* is a wonderful work of photojournalism and a chapter is dedicated to the women war correspondents. In her 1987 book, *Rosie the Riveter Revisited: Women, the War, and Social Change*, Sherna Gluck provides extensive interviews with ten former "Rosies."

For general military history of World War II, two books covering the western theaters are recommended: Charles MacDonald's, *The Mighty Endeavor: American Armed Forces in the European Theater in World War II* and W. G. F. Jackson's *Battle for North Africa.* The D-Day invasion is the topic of Max Hasting's *Overlord: D-Day and the Battle for Normandy.* Biographies of Eisenhower include Stephen Ambrose's *Supreme Commander: The War Years of General Dwight D. Eisenhower* and David Eisenhower's *Eisenhower: At War, 1943-1945.* Ronald Spector's *Eagles Against the Sun* and John Costello's *The Pacific War, 1941-1945* cover the Asian theater. William Manchester's biographies of Winston Churchill and Douglas MacArthur are popular and available in book stores. Samuel Eliot Morison's fifteen-volume history of naval operations will not be equaled, particularly since he was a Navy officer during the War, retiring from the Navy with the rank of Rear Admiral, and later retiring from Harvard University with the rank of Professor Emeritus of American History. Similarly, Churchill's six-volume history of the war will never be out-of-date and provides a good study in executive war-time decision-making.

Index

ALSO FROM THE MINERVA CENTER

BAPTISM OF FIRE

"In this high tech, science fiction novel, Linda Grant De Pauw has come up with a cracking good story. There is mystery, suspense, a hint of romance and victory of the spirit as Maggie Steele develops from an inexperienced young officer into a poised woman commander.

Read the book!"
      --Evelyn P. Foote, Brigadier General, USA (Ret.)

AN UNCOMMON SOLDIER

The Civil War Letters of
Sarah Rosetta Wakeman
Alias Private Lyons
Wakeman
153rd Regiment, New York
State Volunteers
edited by
Lauren Cook Burgess
*with a Foreword by James
M.McPherson*
            "Highly Recommended"
                  --Library Journal